History of Eritrea

From ancient Times up to Independence

Text Book

August 2012

Content
Preface

5

- ELF: Organizational Structure and Leadership (1961-1965)
- Military Developments in the Eritrean Field
- Haile Selassie's Initial Diplomatic and Military Policies
- The Eritrean Liberation Movement (Haraka) in the Field

Lesson 27: The Era of Zonal/Regional Commands (1965-1968)

- The Establishment of the Zonal Commands
- The Consequence of the Zonal Command Era

Lesson 28: Ethiopia's Political and Military Campaigns

- Public Resistance and Ethiopian Conspiracy
- Ethiopia's Scorched-earth Campaign

Lesson 29: The Rectification Movement (Islah, in Arabic)

- The Origins of the Rectification Movement (Islah)
- The Anseba Conference
- The Adobha Conference

Lesson 30: Question and Discussion Time

Lesson 31: The Eritrean People's Liberation Forces [hereafter EPLF]: Birth and Growth

- E.P.L. Forces: First Group
- EPL Forces: Second Group
- Third Group: Eritrean Liberation Forces (Ubel)
- The Merger of the three Groups
- The Civil War and the Establishment of the EPL Forces
- The End of the Civil War

Lesson 32: The Eritrean Revolution at a Turning Point (1974-1977)

- Eritrean Revolution and the fall of the Haile Sellasie Regime
- The Dergue and Governmental Terror
- Flow of tegadelti into the Eritrean Revolution
- The Issue of Unity and the Breaking of the Foreign Mission from the EPLF

Preface

"The History of Eritrea: from Ancient Times up to Independence" is only an outline prepared for the teaching of Eritrean history to students of the Warsay-Yikealo School (Sawa) in particular. At first it was designed as a course prospectus for teachers and reference handbook for students. But realizing its significance as an elementary Eritrean history book to youth outside Sawa, and principally those in the Defense Forces and Diaspora, it is now being published in a book format.

A deeply researched history of Eritrea, from ancient times up to the present, has not yet been written. A big national endeavor therefore awaits Eritrean scholars who need to grow both in number and in kind, and record our history through extensive researches in History, Archeology, Anthropology, Linguistics, etc. And continued efforts are necessary to produce educated Eritrean youth who can live up to this task. In this context, we believe this elementary book will play a modest role in triggering an interest in the history of the Eritrean people.

This work is only a skeleton and needs to be supplemented with additional reference materials. Hence, reference to the following books can be made at every chapter:

1. **Hatsir Tarik Hzbi Ertra**
2. **Hatsir Tarik Bretawi Qalsi**
3. **Megzaeti Italia Ab Ertra**
4. **Aynfelale**
5. **Federeshn Ertra Ms Ityopia**
6. **Sewra Ertra "Msgwamn Mnqulqualn"**
7. **Guezo Kab Naqfa Nab Naqfa**
8. **Klte Kne Ab Dfeat**
9. **Ertrawyan Komando**
10. **Shadushay Werar Bkartun**
11. **Kab Oromay Nab Oromay**

Lesson 1:

The Meaning and Significance of History

Lesson Goals:

At the end of the lesson, students are expected to achieve basic understanding of the following points:

1. Comprehensive meaning of history
2. Significance of history
3. The use and abuse of history

The Meaning of History

- **Even though giving a simple meaning of history is not possible, it is possible to give a comprehensive meaning of history.**

- **History means the story of human beings. It tells *about* what human beings performed in the past. Therefore, all societies and peoples have *a* history. Generally history can be defined using two *approaches*:**

    - **Actual History:***is the process* as it existed and happened. Past actual events, episodes, deeds; government, people, and leaders that appeared; social, political, and economic activities and changes that *took place*... etc.

    - **Documented History:** *is an* actual history documented through research and evidence. <u>Example</u>: The Armed

11

Struggle of the people of Eritrea can be seen as *a* documented history, about the actual history.

The Significance of History

- Even though this short presentation is restrictive on the significance of history, it is possible to list the following points:

History as a tool to understand current events:

- History is a starting point *that helps* us understand the current events of societies because it explains *thedevelopmental* phases that societies passed through; the changes and continuities in political, social, and economic forms they achieved. A*bove all, it is the collective* manners and identities they reflect, thoughts they created, legal and political ideologies, as well as religion and faith.

- History also aids to understand economic activities that societies developed; peaceful and repulsive relationships they had with other societies; and intra-societal relationships within the society and its individual members.

History to anticipate the future

- People always think and fuss about their origin and destination at an individual as well as at communal level. Thus, seen from some part of it, knowledge, interest, and excitement of the past intermingles with the *fear and anxiety* of the future.

- As one well-known historian said, "the reason that a modern person looks back to its dawn of origin with interest is because he hopes that the faint illumination of past decades may enlighten his dim future". *The reason* that humans take interest in history is to get the wisdom that helps them identify and shape their future.

History in maintaining identity and pedestal for *self-esteem*

- History enables a society to maintain its identity by revealing the roots of its origin and culture; educating mores, traditions, and

12

culture. It also makes individuals and societies proud of their identity and history by glorifying *their connection* to history. *Self-esteem* is a wisdom that makes a society move forward.

History as a source of inspiration

- In order to accomplish significant task, to get away from existing stress and misery, to renew the spirit of resistance, to preserve *self-esteem*, and to build self-confidence, societies and individuals need models and inspirations. By recognizing significant accomplishments, *important national heroes*, *dedicated citizens*, and *scientists,* history can serve as *amodel* and source of *inspiration*.

History to identity strengths and *weaknesses*

- In order *for* humans to achieve an all-dimensional progress, they must continuously correct their mistakes and hold on to their strengths. In this regard, recalling history is fundamental. Not knowing history means not progressing.

- As the Roman writer Cicero said, "Not to know what happened before you were born is to be a child forever. For what is the time of a man, except it be interwoven with that memory of ancient things of a superior age?"*Thus,* history and progress have a direct logical link.

Abusing History

- Contradictory to what we have seen above, as to the meaning and significance of history, individuals, groups, and governments use history for inappropriate purposes.

- For example, in order to justify European colonial expansion, *a skewed* version of history was *developed* that provided ground for dominance and colonization. *It was created* to destroy the *self-esteem* of the colonized people, and *fill* their *minds* with the superiority of their colonizers.

13

- The story written by the colonizers told on one hand that *the colonized people had* absolutely no history, never experienced any civilization, lived in the dark ages, and as such, confined them to European colonization; and on the other hand, it *attempted* to show Europeans have a *civilizing* mission for the uncivilized society. The story served the objectives of exploitation, manipulation and domination.

- As an example of this kind of history, let us mention what the philosopher George Hegel, in his "The Philosophy of History" had said the following about Africa: "At this point *we leave Africa, not to mention it again. For it is no historical part of the World; it has no movement or development to exhibit. Historical movements in it—that is in its northern part—belong to the Asiatic or European World. Carthage displayed there an important transitionary phase of civilization; but, as a Phoenician colony, it belongs to Asia. Egypt will be considered in reference to the passage of the human mind from its Eastern to its Western phase, but it does not belong to the African Spirit. What we properly understand by Africa, is the Unhistorical, Undeveloped Spirit, still involved in the conditions of mere nature, and which had to be presented here only as on the threshold of the World's History.*" This kind of abused history and its implication played a significant role in the expansion and establishment of European colonization.

- Even in our national history, as an example, there is a wrong and *skewed* history. In order *to maintain* their *domination* over the people of modern Ethiopia and Eritrea, in order to find out religious and historical reasons for their authority, successive Ethiopian rulers had designed myths that resemble *true history*.

- The myths of Ethiopian rulers *trace* their history and ancestors going back to three thousand years and connecting them with King Solomon and Queen of *Sheba*, and they try to convince *readers* that their Semitic race is 'pure' and their kingdom is blessed by

14

God. However, the fact is that there is limited connection between the ancient civilization that existed in our region before them, and the *20ᵗʰ century history of Ethiopian rulers*.

- **Attention:** As we have seen above, history can be used for constructive and destructive purposes.

Questions:

1. What is history?
2. What are the stages used to define history? Explain them.
3. History can be abused to serve the purpose of the minority. Explain using examples.

Lesson 2:

Prehistoric Eritrea and the Origin of the people of Eritrea

Lesson Goals:

At the end of the lesson, students are expected to achieve basic understanding of the following points:
1. *Prehistoric* **Eritrea**
2. **The origin of the people of Eritrea**

Prehistoric Eritrea

- **<u>Reminder:</u>** First, when we talk about *prehistoric* Eritrea, it should be understood that we would not be limited to the current political boundary of Eritrea. Eritrea, like all African countries, is the product of European colonization. Therefore, when we discuss the pre and post historic Eritrea and *thereafter* up to the coming of Italian colonization, it should be clear that we are discussing the history of our country Eritrea and the *surrounding regions.*
- According to the archeological research made so far, the Great Rift Valley of East Africa has been confirmed to bethe origin of the human race. It should be understood that Eritrea, as part of this region, is also the origin of man. The over one million-years old human skeleton found in Buya, Denkalia, is one evidence.

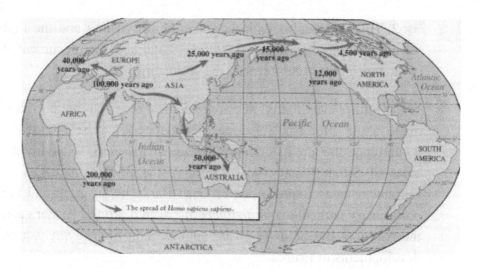

The Spread of Homo Sapiens from their original home, the East African Rift Valley

- The fact that before about *1,000* years, the first Homo sapiens travelled from Africa to Asia through the '***Bab El mended***' canal makes it clear that Eritrea was the origin and bridge of humans.

The Evolution of Man

- History is classified into two:

    1. Pre-history: This part of history begins from the appearance of human beings in the planet and continues up for *tens* of thousands of years ending with the invention of writing, ***which is about 5,000*** years ago.

2. History: begins with the invention of writing and the first civilizations that began 5,000 years ago and was documented in writing. It is shorter than the prehistoric era.

- In the future, even though the archeological research that has been made about prehistoric Eritrea is understood to be broad and continuing; the prehistoric *archeological artifacts* found in the areas of Silum Beaati (near Tserona), the prehistoric traces of settlement areas found in lower Gash Barka to Akurdet; and the preliminary archeological *artifacts* discovered around Asmara and the banks of the Setit River are enough indicators of prehistoric developments in Eritrea.

Prehistoric Cave Paintings at Silum Beaati, Eritrea

The *Origin* of the People of Eritrea

- The people of Eritrea are the result of the *mixing* of different people over a long period of time. The mixing of Nilotic, Cushitic, and Semitic blood that came about by migration, *marriage*, and war. This mixed composition has left *a* significant signature in the cultures and internal relationships of the people of Eritrea.

18

- **Reminder:** As mentioned above, the people of Eritrea *are* people that have Nilotic, Cushitic, and Semitic origins. However, it is important to raise the question, "what is the basis for the classification into 'Nilotic, Cushitic, and Semitic'?" Many people think this kind of classification is racist. This is a wrong thinking. First, humans have only one race. However, even though *humans belong to one race*, on one hand there are *physical and external features* such as the *color and tone of the skin*, and on the other hand, from *culture to language there are differences*. Based on culture and language, *people* have classifications. This classification, however, is ethnic not racial.

- Therefore, it is important to understand that when the people of Eritrea are classified into categories, it is based on ethnicity, not race. Moreover, it is important to understand that through a process that took many years, the people of Eritrea have intermixed and interconnected. Nonetheless, based on culture and language, it is possible to *classify them* into the following three ethnic categories.

  1. **Nilotic language originspeakers**: Kunama and Nara
  2. **Cushitic language originspeakers**: Bilen, Hidarb, Saho, and Afar.
  3. **Semitic language origin speakers**: Tigrigna, Tigre, and Rashyda

Questions:

1. Which part of the world is the origin of humans?
2. List the important prehistoric places in Eritrea.
3. What are the factors used as a base to categorize the people of Eritrea into ethnic groups?

Lesson 3:

Ancient History of Eritrea up to the 7th century *CE*

Lesson Goals:

At the end of the lesson, students are expected to achieve basic understanding of the following points:

- Pre-Axum civilization
- The emergence, advancement, and decline of the *Axumite* Kingdom (1st – 7th century CE)

Historical Developments before the *Axumite* Civilization

A. Punt Land: 2,500 B*CE*

- As can be learned from ancient Egyptian records and new genetic-based researches, from around 2,500 years ago, there was a great kingdom around the Red Sea coast called the **Land of Punt** with its center at the port of Adulis, extending to the Northern parts of modern up to *The* Sudan and in the South up to Djibouti. *The* Egyptians called it the *Land of God. The* kingdom of Punt had firmly established commercial and cultural relationships with *the Egyptians and Phoenicians* (who had established *a* civilization in the Eastern Coast of *The Mediterranean* Sea). This was around 1,000 BC. The kingdom was exporting ivory, gold, aromatic resins, ebony, *men and women slaves*, leather, and domestic as well as wild animals. *It was also* importing commercial items, such as grapes, bronze, and nickel.

B. The Kingdom of Deamat (8th century *BCE*)

- From *around 1,000 BCE* people *called Sabaeans* came to Eritrea crossing from Southern Arabia, and settled first in *The Dahlak*

Islands and later in the *seashores* and highlands of Eritrea. *They later settled in places* such as Adulis, Kohayto, Tekonda, Keskese, and Metera. Around the 8th century BCE, the Deamat Dynasty including all *these* towns was established.

- Adulis was the center of this Kingdom; from Adulis it extended its reach to Axum. In these areas, the Sabaeans made a significant contribution to the development of agriculture, architecture, political system, language, religion and faith. Since the Kingdom of Deamat was the dominant kingdom in this area, it was able to establish commercial and cultural *relationships* with the Greeks, the Roman Empire, and the kingdom of *Meroe* (Present *day* Sudan).

The *Emergence* of the *Axumite* Kingdom (1st Century CE)

- The *Axumite* Kingdom was the continuation and culmination of all former civilizations in the area. It was *established* in the 1st century CE, pulling together the towns of Adulis, Kohayto, Keskese, Tekonda, Metera, and Axum.

An Ancient Reservoir at SafiraThe Stele at Metera

21

A. Historical Turning Points that Identify the *Axumite* Kingdom

- Fundamental reform in architecture and *The Geez* language

- Introduction of monetary economy

- Development of religious books written in Geez, artistic works, philosophical explanations, medical books, musical and poetry books, scientific writings, dictionary and grammar books, and astronomical books.

- Before the introduction of Christianity in the 4th century CE, the people of these areas were polytheistic. For example, their prominent gods they believed in were gods of the sun, the moon, the sea, and the land.

- However, in the first half of the 4th century CE, a Syrian *monk* by the *name* Freminatos preached Christianity in the *Axumite* Kingdom. It took many years for the Christian faith to take ground and *be a dominant religion*. It was after the coming of nine preachers also called the nine saints, among whom were Abune (Father) Yehani, Abune Libanos, and Abune Zemichael (better known by Abune aregawi), following Abune Freminatos and *served for many years* preaching Christianity were able to *overcome the existing* faiths and established Christianity as the dominant religion. *With the passing of time*, the religious rituals that existed before the introduction of Christianity disappeared. *Nevertheless*, they had left their linguistic and ritualistic marks *on* Christianity. For example, the word *Egizabher* (commonly used for God in Geez and Tigrigna) *came out of the* pre-Christian religion and *from a god of the sky* and the land called 'Bhier or Meharem'.Monument Axumite

22

- The expansion of the *Axumite* Kingdom: at one time *the* Axumite Kingdom had *extended its influence* and reach up to the Nile River by conquering the Meroe Kingdom to its *Northwest*. To the South, it reached up to the Land of Agew (Ethiopia), and crossing the sea, it had established its rule in South Arabia (Yemen).

The Decline of the *Axumite* Kingdom

Beginning from the 7th century, the *Axumite* Kingdom began to decline for the following reasons:

- The Persian invasions of the Arabian Peninsula and the Red Sea
- The interruption of maritime and land commerce, and
- The expansion and invasions of the Beja *kingdom.*

Questions:

1. Mention the kingdoms that existed in this region before the *Axumite* Kingdom.
2. *Identify* the characteristics that distinguish*ed* the *Axumite* Kingdom.
3. In its golden age, *how far did the Axumite Kingdom expand*?
4. List the reasons for the decline of the *Axumite* Kingdom.

Lesson 4:

The Medieval History of Eritrea (8th – 16th Century)

The Medieval History of Eritrea (8th – 16th Century)

Lesson Goals:

At the end of the lesson, students are expected to achieve basic understanding of the following points:

- The Beja Kingdom

- The Beginning and expansion of Islam

- The Invasions of Ahmed Grange

- The coming of the Portuguese and the Ottoman Turks

The Beja Kingdom

- *In the previous lesson* we have *seen* that around the 8th century the Bejas by pushing Southward from the North had played a big role in arresting *Axumite* Kingdom's expansion. Their nomadic life style helped them to easily *expand* their networks from the areas of Hirgigo to Rora Sahel, from Anseba to Barka, including the highlands of Eritrea. *In order to know some* of the Beja Kingdoms that flourished during that time, *we list the following five main ones*:

    1. *Naqis*: This kingdom expanded from Aswan (Southern Egypt) to Lower Barka and included the Hidarb and the Mensa.

2. **_Baqlin_**: This kingdom expanded from Rora to central Barka, and it included pastoralists who lived by looking after their cattle and camel herds.
3. **_Bazin_**: This was formed by the Kunama and Nara people around Barka and the kingdom was mainly of agriculturalists.
4. **_Jarin:_** This kingdom expanded from the port of Massawa to the Barka River, and in the South it expended up to Zayla (in Somalia) including towns like the Dahlak Island.
5. **_Qata_** (Qota): This Beja kingdom expanded from the border of Massawa up to Faylum (No one knows where this place is).

- The Beja kingdom ended around the 13th century. However, its legacy lives on in traditions and archaeological remains. For example, among **the** Tigre they still tell about **a fierce nomadic fighters called** 'Rome' (which means Beja), and Tigrigna **folklore that mentions** the 'Belew Kelew', shows the influence and power of the Bejas.

The *Coming* and Expansion of Islam

A 7th Century Arabic Script engraved on stone
Found in the Dahlak Island

25

Around 610 CE, *The* Prophet Mohammed began preaching Islam in Arabia. However, he got strong opposition from the Quraysh tribe who *were profiting* from the previous religion. *The* Prophet Mohammed advised some of his early followers to seek a secure refuge from the assassination and imprisonment they were facing from the opposition. Thus, they came into our region because the political and religious tradition in Eritrea was one of tolerance. The first 15-17 followers, including the daughter of *The* Prophet Mohammed, came to Eritrea in 615 CE seeking sanctuary. After that, in the second and third wave of migration over 100 joined them.

- This way, Islam was introduced *into* Eritrea without any military confrontation. This historical event makes Eritrea the first country in Africa *that Islam was introduced as a religion.*

- The second way *Islam came into Eritrea was by way of commerce.* Particularly, in the 8th century, from 702 to 725, the Umayyad Dynasty, to *expand its trade circle took control* of the Red Sea and *Arabian* Peninsula. *At this time s*ome Moslems settled in the Dahlak islands, and they gradually expanded to Massawa. *The* makes the Dahlak Islands the gateway *of Islam* into Eritrea.

- Islam, up to the 10th century, was limited in The Dahlak Islands, Red Sea coast, and the Gulf of Aden. After the 10th century, that means after the Fatimid *Dynasty* came *into* Egypt, and since the situation in the Red Sea region became relatively peaceful, commercial activity was reactivated and the influence of Islam in our region increased. In the 12-13th century, a free Islamic Kingdom that *ran* vigorous maritime commerce was established in Dahlak Islands. Its traces are still present.

The Invasions of Ahmed *Grange* and the coming of the Portuguese and the Turkish Empire

- In the first half of the 16th century, an Imam by the name Ahmed *Grange* of Adal attacked the Kingdom of Amhara, and expanded to the different parts of Amhara, and the highlands of Eritrea, that were under the rule of the Kingdom of Medri-Bahri (Land of the Sea). King Libnedengel of Amhara, unable to resist the number and power of Grange's troops requested the support of the Portuguese. In 1541, the Portuguese landed in Massawa to rescue King Gelawdyos (son of King Libnedengel). For his part, Ahmed *Grange* asked the Ottoman *Turks* to help him and he got 900 armed troops and artillery. In *1554*, the *alliances* of King Libnedengel of Amhara, Bahri-Negassi (King) Isaac of highland Eritrea, and the Portuguese defeated *Grange's army. Grange was hit in the chest, fell down, and died!*

Grange Soldiers Attacking

- Under this circumstance, beginning from the first *16th* century, the Red Sea coast came under *the* control of the *Ottoman Turks or*

Ottoman Empire. For example, in 1517 the Turkish brought Suakin and Massawa under their control. However, the Turkish were only governing Massawa *by* proxy, using local chiefs of Belew, *originally* known by the title the *Turks gave them:* 'Naib'. In 1557, after forty years, the *Turks* sent their army into Massawa, and starting from there they moved up to the highlands and controlled Debarwa, *which* was capital of Bahri-Negassi Isaac. Bahri-Negassi Isaac took counter *offensive* measures *by mobilizing the people and defeated the Turks*. Three years later, Bahri-Negassi Isaac refused to pay *taxes* to King Minnassie of Amhara and a confrontation ensued. Bahri-Negassi Isaac sought help in order to fight and *defeat* Minnasie, and he asked the Turks for help. They *came to assist him and* stood on his side. However, the Amhara prevailed and the alliances of Bahri-Negassi Isaac and *the Turks lost*, and Bahri-Negassi Isaac died in the battle.

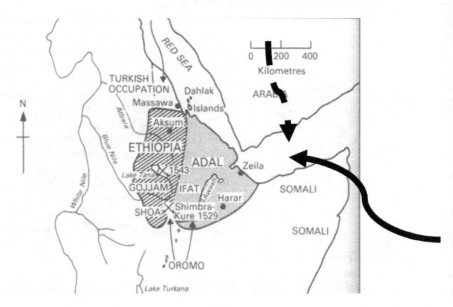

Map Showing the Expansion of the Portuguese and Turks in the Horn of Africa

Questions:

1. *Which ones were the main Beja kingdoms?* Identify the areas they were controlling.
2. How is *the coming and* expansion of *Islam* different in Eritrea from *the* other parts *in the area?*
3. Explain the role of international powers (Portuguese and Turkish) in this region.

Lesson 5:

The State of *Modern* Eritrea between the *17ᵗʰ* - *19ᵗʰ* Century

---

Lesson Goals:

At the end of the lesson, students are expected to achieve basic understanding of the following points:

- They will have an idea about the political developments of the mid*17ᵗʰ* -*19ᵗʰ* century.

The Highlands of Eritrea

- *Around the mid 17ᵗʰ -19ᵗʰ century*, the highland area called 'Medri-Bahri' or 'Mereb-Melash' was ruled from Debarwa by the Bahri Negestat (Kings of the Sea). Based on the balance of power, it had an up and down relationship with the Kings of Amhara and *Tigray.*
- In the *17ᵗʰ* century, when the power and authority of the Medri-Bahri began to wane due to the opposition of the Amhara Kingdom, a group of *highland* individuals emerged claiming the right to rule the highlands. Up to the end of the *18ᵗʰ* century, they formed a system that had a kinship structure. For example, in the first part of the 17ᵗʰ century, a man from Hamasien called Tesfatsion Ateshem of Adi Qontsi ruled the entire Hamasien *region*.

The Red Sea Coast

- Beginning the 10th century this part of Eritrea *was* under the control of the Turks, and it was ruled from Hirgigo and Massawa by the viceroys of *the Turks.*
- The people of Afar *were* composed of two clans: the Ademara & the Asamara, *and* was being ruled by its own Sultans.
- The people of Saho had no *master-servant* relationships. *They were administered* by elected Councils.

The Western Lowlands

- In different periods, the Western Lowland of Eritrea *wasunder several* different kingdoms. For example, in around the *14th* century, it was under the Belew Kingdom that ruled from Suakin to the Gash River. Beginning the *16th* century, it was under the Sudanese Kingdom of Funji. The Kingdom of Funji put some of the tribes of Tigre and Beja collectively under its deputies called Nabtab. The ruler of Nabtab had the title of Deglel.

The Nara and Kunama

- Nara and Kunama as *non-stratified* society (undivided into servant and master) were governed by their own councils. This period can be considered as the darkest time for Nara and Kunama. The nonstop and continuous attack and plunder by the Kings of Amhara and Tigray *left* a visible scar of *demographic and economic damage. Because of this*, the number of the populations of these two people had *dropped multiple folds*. The agony of that period is still alive in their *memories and history*.

The Bilen

- After the decline of the *Axumite* Kingdom, between the *10th through the 13th centuries*, and because of the escalating political unrest in the land of Agew, many Agew migrated to Eritrea to get a secure sanctuary. *The Bilen* of Eritrea is the remnant of this migration. As soon as they came in, they become the masters of the local people, whom they *met* there.

- In Sahel, the highlanders (the biet Asghede) who came from Tsinadegle by way of Adi Nifas established a serf-master relationship over the people they found in Sahel. This feudal system that was led by the Kentibay of biet Asghede persisted as is until the 1940s. The serf-master relationship in the Mariya, Mensae, and Belien was active in full force until the 1940s. However, after the serf rebellion of the 1940s the system was weakened and was replaced by the rule of tribal chiefs.

- As a result the coming of the Egyptians, in some of its aspects was seen as deliverance to those people who were suffering from continuous raids and plunders in the hands of the feudal warlords of Tigray.

Questions:
1. *How was the relationship* between the highlands of Eritrea, the rulers of Amhara, and Tigray?
2. Where was the center of the Fuji kingdom?
3. Why was this period the most malevolent era for the people of Nara and Kunama?

Lesson 6:

Question and Discussion Period

> **Discussion in groups**
> - Every classroom forms groups, with each group electing a chairperson and secretary and discussing on assigned topics. A summary of the discussion is then presented to the class.
> - Assuming a period is 60 minutes long, 25 minutes are allocated for the discussion part and the remaining 35 minutes for the group presentations.

Points for discussion (to be answered in groups):

1. What is the significance of learning Eritrean history?

2. What is the difference between prehistory and history?

3. There is only one human race. Give pro or con arguments to this.

4. Can the history of Axum be the sole property of only one country Eritrea or Ethiopia?

5. What was the significance of the sea ports in the introduction of religion in our area?

6. What do you know about the invasion of Tigrean and Amhara warlords in our oral traditions?

Lesson 7:

The Invasions of the Egyptians and the *Royalists of Tigray*

Lesson Goals:

At the end of the lesson, students will learn:

- On one hand, the *offensives* of the Egyptians and the feudal *warlords of Tigray*, and on the other hand, the counter response of the people of Eritrea.

The Offensives carried out by Egypt

- Egypt was under the Ottoman Empire. As we have seen earlier, the Red Sea coast of Eritrea was under **Turkish rule**. At the beginning of the mid-19th century, the Ottoman power began to **decline**. On the other hand, under the leadership of Mohammed Ali Pasha, Egyptian began to gain power, **and they** started replacing the Ottoman power. As a proof of this, in 1821 the Egyptians attacked **The Sudan** and overthrew the Funji Kingdom. Next, in 1823 they controlled Sebderat and increased their influence in Western Eritrea. In 1846, they rented Massawa and Hirgigo from the Turks.

- In the first of 1870s, the Egyptians began to intensify their activity to seize the highlands and other parts of Eritrea. This way, in 1872, they took over Bogos (Keren area) and put it under their control. In order to capture the rest of Eritrea's highlands and beyond, in 1875 and 1876, they launched two *offensives*. However, they were defeated **at the battles** of Gundet (1875) and Gura (1876), by the troops of Emperor

Yohannes of Tigray. As a result their military and political *interest* to control the highlands of Eritrea failed. In these two battles, the role and contributions of *Raesi* Woldemichael Solomon of Hazega was magnificent. Since he had captured significant artillery, *his military* power was strengthened more than before, and being confident of this, he challenged Emperor Yohannes. This angered Emperor Yohannes, and in 1878, he dispatched *Raesi* Bayru Ghebretsadik (Aba Gala), to fight Ra'si Woldemichael. The two armies fought in Asmara, with *Raesi* Woldemichael attacking from the east and *Raesi Bayru was killed*. After this victory, *Raesi* Alula deceived *Raesi* Woldemichael into making peace and Ra'si Woldemichael agreed. However, staying in a waylay area; the troops of Emperor Yohannes arrested *Raesi* Woldemichael. *Raesi* Woldemichael spent the rest of his life in prison *at* the monastery of Endaba Selama (Ethiopia).

The *Offensives* of the *Tigray Warlords* and the coming of the Mahdists

• The people of Eritrea, after having being suffered a lot from the invasion and plunders (these two are the inseparable military behaviors of *warlords*) by the Tigrean warlords such as *Degiyat* Wubie, Raesi Alula, and others and *Tigrayans* became more vulnerable. Particularly Alula, after he was *appointed governor* of the Mereb Melash, the attacks and plunders became worse. Even though there was no section of our people that was not affected by the Tigrean attacks, those *who* were affected the most were the people of Nara, Kunama, Saho, and Afar. Though they had put a heroic resistance to defend themselves against the attacks, many people *lost their lives* and significant *economic assets were destroyed*. The people of Sahel, Bilen, Mensae, Bineamer, and the people of highland Eritrea became victims of these continuous

Tigrean attacks. Moreover, departing from *The Sudan,* the Mahdists (also called Durbushes) made the people, especially the people of Barka, subject to attacks and plunders.

- In the first mid of the 19th century, because of the repetitive attacks, the expansion of the Egyptians, and the weakening of the Orthodox Church, the people of Bilen, Maria Keyeh and Tselim, Mensae, Bet-Juk, and Bet-Asghede, who up to that time were followers of the Orthodox Church, converted to Islam, *Catholicism, and Lutheranism.*

Questions:

1. Why did Turkey transfer its colony in the Red Sea coast of Eritrea to Egypt?

2. Why did the Egyptians attempt to conquer the highlands and beyond *fail?*

3. Explain the distribution and consequences of the offensives *carried out by royalists of Tigray* in Eritrea.

4. Who *were* the Mahdists?

Lesson 8:

The *Beginning* and Expansion of Italian Colonization

Lesson Goals:

At the end of the lesson, students will learn:

How the Italian colonization that made Eritrea to get its current political structure began, the social, economic, and political situation in Eritrea, and the expansion and settlement of Italian *colonists*.

The *Beginning* of Italian Colonization

- The political and economic **situations** that dominated Eritrea during that time **had created conducive conditions for the plan of Italian colonization to conquer the land**. As we saw in the previous lesson, the people of Eritrea, especially in the second mid of the 19th century, **were** weakened by the continuous and repetitive offensives and abductions, and **the power of their** resistance was drained. Moreover, in 1888, **due to the great** draught and famine **that took place in** the Horn of Africa, the people of Eritrea **were affected** by the great famine. Thus, these two reasons, unlike the challenges that other colonial powers faced, made it relatively easier for **the coming** of Italian colonization.

- First, in 1869, Italy through a Catholic monk by the name Giuseppe Sapeto, and on behalf of **an Italian trading** company called Rubattino rented Assab from its Sultanate. After 13 years the company transferred Assab into the direct control of the Italian government. Next, in 1885, it controlled Beylul, and in February *of 1885 it controlled* Massawa displacing Egypt. This shows the beginning of Italian colonization in Eritrea also followed the typical *way colonialism works*, through *trading* companies, missionaries, and discoverers.

Expansion

- After *the* Italians took over Massawa, in 1887 they built camps *at* Sa'ati and Wiaa. Many traditional leaders of the people of Eritrea, who were tired of the attacks of the Tigray warlords, *and being bruised and weakened* by the great famine, began to move *to the Italian side* hoping to get Italian support and protection. For example, Kentibay Hamid of Sahel and all those who had taken refuge in Sahel from Tigrean warlords' attack were the first to welcome Italian coming to Eritrea.

- However, the expansion of Italian *colonialism* was not without resistance. As we saw before, the *warlords* of Tigray, and especially Emperor Yohannes, had direct colonial *interests* in Eritrea. Since the expansion of Italy directly *affected* his interest, it was natural for a confrontation to appear between these two colonial powers. Thus, *on* January 25, 1887, Raesi Alula *of Tigrayled an army* and attacked the Italian army that was posted *at* Sa'ati. However he didn't succeed. The next day, he destroyed one unit of *an* Italian army at Dogalli. The defeat of the Italians at Dogalli by an African army did not only frustrate and *shame* the Italians, it also *affected other* Europeans. However, Alula did not continue the war. One year later, Emperor Yohannes and *Alula*, went to northwestern Ethiopia to fight off the expansion of the Mahdists from the Sudan. In 1889, the Mahdists killed Emperor Yohannes *at the battle of* Mettema.

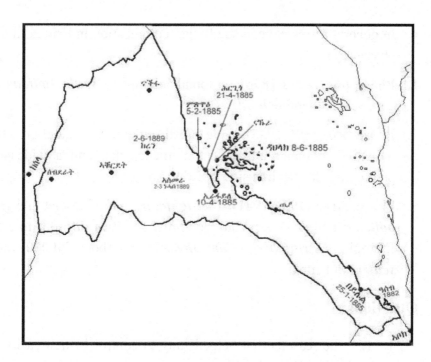

Italian Expansion in Eritrea

- The encirclement of Emperor Yohannes and Alula (in the South by Menelik, and in the Northwest by the Mahdists) provided *a great* opportunity for the Italians. *T*hey continued expanding their territory. In 1889 they took over Keren and Asmara. After few months they controlled the *entire highlands* up to the Mereb River. After this, *on* January 1, 1890, they declared their occupied territory a colony and gave it the name "Eritrea". With this modern Eritrea was born as a country.

- While the Italians put Eritrea under their *colonial control*, Emperor Menelik of Shewa, taking advantage of the death of Emperor Yohannes, put the people of Oromo, Guragie, Aderie, Afar, Somali, and Wolayta under the *colonial administration of Shewa*. Therefore, *the two* countries, Eritrea through Italian colonization, and Ethiopia through the feudalist invasions of Emperor Menelik, were formed almost at the same period.

- In general *terms* we can see Italian colonization in Eritrea in three phases:

1. **Phase one (1890-1896):** colonial attempt to *settle Italians* and confiscate all arable *land.*

2. **Phase two (1896-1935):** widespread settlement, gradual growth of industrial, commercial and economic capital, and a widespread preparation for the invasion of Ethiopia.

3. **Phase three (1935-1941):** the *tightening* up of fascist and racist *policies*; and a widespread economic activities in order to attack Ethiopia. D*uringthis period there* were about 70,000 Italian *settlers* in Eritrea.

Questions:

1. List the reasons that helped Italy to control Eritrea easily and without strong opposition.
2. Mention the basic aims of Italian colonization.

Lesson 9:

Opposition against Italian Colonization

Lesson Goals:

At the end of this lesson, students will learn:

- Examples of Eritreans who *roseup* against Italian colonization.
- As we have seen earlier, except the resistance of the people of Afar in 1881 and 1885, there was no significant resistance to mention that the people of Eritrea made against the *coming* of Italian colonization. This was due to the fact that *Eritreans were* weakened by warfare and *had seen* Italian colonization as a better solution. *Many* Eritrean traditional leaders (appointees) went to Massawa and sought protection from Italy.

Italian Reaction to Eritrean Resistance: Assassination and *Incarceration* of Traditional Leaders

- The *peaceful looking welcome it received from Eritreans made* Italy uncomfortable. It knew that eventually its colonization would face opposition, as a result it started *disbanding* all perceived opponents and opposition leaders. Because of this, between 1889 and 1890, about 800 traditional leaders and their followers *were* killed, and many more were imprisoned in Assab and Nakura.

The Notorious Italian Prison at the Island of Nakura

The *Uprising* of Eritrean people against Italy

- As expected, when Italy began confiscating *land, assassinating people*, and arresting traditional leaders, it met *resistance* from all corners of Eritrea. Heroes who made impression and honor in the minds of the people appeared from *the areas of* Saho, Binamer, Denkel, Kunama, Nara, and *the* highlands. For example:

  o Zemat wed Ikud, Bulunyan, and Dember Aga from Barka
  o ***Beromberas*** Kafil Gofar from Dembelas
  o Ali Mohammed ***Osman*** Burri (Nakura prison breaker) from Afar
  o Degiyat Abera Hailu, acclaimed by Emperor Menelik of Ethiopia by the Amharic phrase: "Keshi Amara, and Abera" (One Abera better than a thousand Amhara) from Hamasien.
  o Degiyat Mahray (Nakura prison brea)

Degiyat Kafil of Dembelas   Zemat wed Ikud of Barka

- o Kentibay Hamid of Habab
- o Degiyat Bahta Hagos (Babene Bahta Hagos) who got the highest recognition in the history of the *uprising from Akele Guzai*
- o Abubeker Ahmmed and Mohammed Nuri from Saho
- o Sultan Yassin Haysema from Afar

Let us mention some of them *in detail* because they have impressive and inspiring history, and they have important place in the people's memory.

Kentibay Hamid of Habab

43

Degiyat Bahta Hagos

- Of all the *oppositions* made against Italian colonization, the biggest was the one staged by Degiyat Bahta Hagos. After the Italians occupied Massawa, Bahta Hagos welcomed them and had accepted their protection and assistance. From this he was able to strengthen his troops by getting arms from them. Since Degiyat Bahta Hagos had killed a Tigraean warlord, he was forced to seek *a sanctuary* for himself and his troops from Kentibay Hammd of Sahel. In 1889, following the occupation of the highlands, the Italians appointed Degiyat Bahta *as a governor of Segenyti*. However, Degiyat Bahta Hagos was not happy. In 1893, Italy decided to expropriateone fifth of *the highland's* farming land. Next, they *doubled the area of land they had previously seized*. This meant they had almost expropriated the entire *highland's arable land*. Bahta was extremely angry. His suspicion of the Italians, *was better conveyed by the following dirge to his brother, Sengal:*

Degiyat Bahta Hagos

44

> My brother Sengal do not be too foolish,
> My brother Sengal do not be too foolish,
> If a white snake bites, *you can't find medicine for its venom.*

- On December 1894, Bahta declared his *revolt against the Italians*. Together with his brother Sengal and his son Ghebremedhin, he imprisoned an Italian commander *named Lieutenant Giovanni Sanguinetti*. After this, Bahta tried to *march over the entire highlands*. He wrote a letter to the traditional leaders of Asawurta and Seraye, and on December 16, he made a speech *at a meeting and stated*, "I will liberate you from the one *who* came from overseas to take our rights, seize our lands, expropriate our agriculture, and *destroy* our forest."

- On December 18, Bhata attacked an Italian army *stationed at Halay*. He *caused* a huge damage. In the same night, *the Italians sent a reinforcement force and the balance of power shifted*. Bhata *was* wounded and *later died as a martyr with immense heroism*.

Escape from Nakura: an Amazing Testament of Determination and Courage

- During the Italian occupation, Nakura as a prison island was a sign of colonial atrocity and oppression. In this isolated and *desolate island*, nationalist Eritreans who opposed and suspected of opposing Italian colonization, were detained and most of them were dying from miserable living *conditions*. It was under this circumstance that in the history of Eritrean opposition to Italian colonization the incredible incident of Nakura prison break took place. This incident happened *on* 17 November, 1899. During that time, in the island, there were 27 guards and two Italian commanders, and around 119 prisoners. *On that day*, 12 prisoners with six guards were sent to fetch water from the nearby well. *When they* reached there, the *prisoners* took the weapons of their guards killing one of the Italian guard and taking the other hostage. They broke into the prison and freed 107

45

prisoners, and took the captured *Italians*, six Eritrean guards, and the 107 prisoners to Bure peninsula. Some of those Eritreans who escaped from Nakura include Ali Mohammed Osman Buri (referred in the Afar language as 'Nakura yagali', which literally means breaker of Nakura), Degiyat Mahri (best remembered by the song: *Mahraye, Mahraye, he is gone by parting the lake*), and Bilata Ghebre'ezgiabher Gilamariam.

Questions:

1. Mention the *stepsthe Italians* took to prevent *any possible* opposition *from the Eritrean people?*

2. Why did not the collaboration among Eritrean traditional leaders take much time to develop into opposing *Italian colonization?*

3. Give examples of Eritrean opposition to Italian colonization?

Lesson 10:

Economic activities of Italian Colonization

Lesson Goals:

At the end of this lesson, students will achieve basic understanding of:

- The economic activities of Italian colonization and the introduction of colonial economic capital *into* Eritrea.

Generally speaking, in Eritrea, the objectives of Italian colonial *policies* were

1. Repatriating Italian poor farmers and victims of social outcasts *into* Eritrea.

2. Using Eritrea as a source of raw materials, and as a market for the finished products of Italian *industrialists.*

3. Using Eritrea as a springboard for additional colonial expansion (especially *into* Ethiopia).

- However, since directly and indirectly economic development was required to achieve the stated objectives and policies, Italian colonization began to invest in different economic sectors in Eritrea. Let us see the following examples *so that* we can see how the expansion of the economic *expansion grew*:

A. *Railway*: between the periods of 1887 to 1932 of Italian colonization:

47

- 125 kilometers long railway line from Asmara to Massawa was built

- 104 kilometers long railway line from Asmara to Keren was constructed

- 123 kilometers long railway line from Keren to Akurdet and from Akurdet to Gash was built. In total, *the Italians built 352 kilometers long railway lines in Eritrea.*

The Inauguration of the Massawa-Asmara Railway December 1911

B. Roads: Between 1890 and 1941

- About 710 kilometers long of all-weather roads were built and because of *these all of the* main towns *in Eritrea* were connected.

- In addition, *there were* about 1,500 kilometers long *seasonal roads*, primarily used for military service.

Asmara-Massawa Cableway   Road Construction

C. Cableway:

- Another transportation line that the Italians built was the cableway, which in its time was the longest in the world, and *it* connected Asmara and Massawa. The cableway shortened the Asmara - Massawa road to *be* 71 kilometers, and it had the capacity of transporting 720 tons *of goods* a day.

D. Communication

- In the entire life of the Italian colonization, domestic postal service, over 500 miles long telegraph, and telephone services were constructed. Moreover, in 1935, a regular airlines service began in Eritrea. To facilitate the service, airports were built in Massawa, Asmara, Assab, Tessenei, and Gura.

E. *Sea* Ports

- During Italian colonization, the port *city* of Massawa, having its size and capacity increased, became one of the biggest ports in this region. On the opposite, in Assab, the Italians, let alone to give *it any thought* and make *any investment* comparable to what *they built* in Massawa, they *made no modest attempt to build it. Hence, the port city* of Assab became a killing and imprisonment place for those nationalists who opposed *Italian* colonization.

Massawa Port

F. Education

- The educational policy of Italian colonization for Eritreans was not human development, but to use them as servants of the *colonial administration*. Academic education was limited to grade four *levels,* and some technical training.

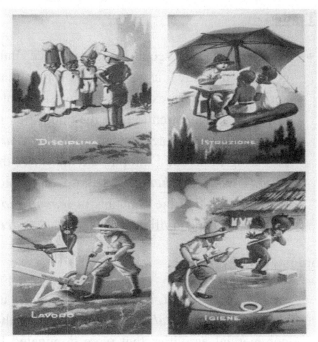

Italian Educational System Goals: Sanitation,

G. <u>Agriculture</u>

- After the settlement program failed, the agricultural policy of Italian colonization *shifted to moving* to agro industrial products, *which demanded more in the markets*. The policy was basically designed to serve Italians only. The fact that the budget of the government was less than 1%; *it was a clear indication* that showed the policy was ineffective. In addition, since forced conscription restricted many Eritrean youth, the agricultural productivity was severely damaged. However, generally speaking, to some extent, Italian colonization contributed to the transformation of Eritrean farming *that changed from* traditional to modern style. Example: domestic animals vaccination, agricultural laboratory, and *the introduction* of modern commercial farming *can be mentioned.*

H. Trade

- In the first and second phases, since Italian colonization considered Eritrea as a source of raw materials and as a springboard for its expansionist invasions into Ethiopia, it did not give much attention to the industrial sector. However, before 1935 and later, and *during the years that Italy* was preparing to invade Ethiopia, the industries that *were attached* to *the invading scheme*, and those economic institutions that partially satisfied the demands of *tens of thousands* of Italian mercenaries and civilian armies showed *fastergrowth.*

I. Industry

Eritrea, because of its strategic location, is convenient for trade. *When the Italians came* to Eritrea they took over the commercial activities that were dominated by a few Indians and others. They began to exploit salt, palm tree, minerals, and others with small investments and capital. After 1935, like all other sectors, trade also developed *rapidly*. In 1939, there was 486 million Lire capital *invested in Eritrea*, and 2,690 commercial companies *flourished in the country*. As stated before, even though the Italians had dominated the markets, there were some Indian, Greece, Arab, and Jewish merchants. Eritreans, *besides owning small groceries*,  were not participating in foreign trade. An Oil Factory during the Italian.

- To conclude *this lesson*, Italian economic activities were a signal of 'colonial economic development'. This kind of economy serves only colonial objectives, and considers the natives as servants rather than beneficiaries. ***Thus, the economy that was built by the Italians was racist and unfair.***

Questions:

1. Explain the objectives of the economic policy of Italian colonization.
2. Briefly explain the achievements the Italian economic activities accomplished in Eritrea.

Lesson 11:

Italian Rule – Its legacies and downfall

Lesson Goals:

At the end of this lesson, students are expected to have the following basic knowledge:

- The economic, military, and administrative policies of Italy, their contributions to the transformation of Eritrean society, and the establishment of nationhood and nationalism
- How and under what circumstances did the Italian rule get replaced by The British Administration

Social and political changes brought by Italian Colonialism

- Before the coming of the Italians, there were not any Eritrean cities, except Massawa. The economic structure of Eritrea was weak, but it was interrelated due to the agrarian and pastoralist nature of the society.

- The existing economic relationship was small and only serving few areas. Except few traders, the rest of Eritreans were living on traditional farming and methods of pastoralism.

- As mentioned above, due to Italian rule, there were some fundamental changes that affected Eritrean society. Within 50 years, the cities of Asmara, Keren, Assab, Akurdet, Dekemhare, Mendefera, and Tessenei were built; communication lines were established; and basic economic structure of nationhood and nationalism were laid over.

- As a result of direct Italian rule, a capitalist economy that employed workers by paying them salaries was formed

- In addition to the economic changes brought by Italian rule, there were military conscriptions, administrative changes, and the codification of laws that helped in the solidification of Eritrean nationalism

- From the time the Italians set their feet in Eritrea, they were using young Eritreans to serve in the army. In 1935, when Italy invaded Ethiopia, the number of Eritrean conscripts was about 60, 000. All of those conscripts who experienced the same level of training and fighting were able to foster a unified sense of belonging to each other and as a result a level of consciousness developed.

- The Italian administration that brought a centralized from of governing and the application of rules, laws, and order created a sense of Eritrean nationalism

The end of Italian colonialism

- As the events of Italian colonialism in Eritrea were the results of the developments in Europe, its end was also tied to the events that developed in Europe

- When World War II started in Europe in 1939, Mussolini was watching the events of the balance of power, and did not take any side until 1940. When Germany scored quick victory over France, Mussolini thought German victory was a final one.

- On June 10, 1940, Mussolini joined his forces with the Axis Powers that was run by Germany and Japan, and declared war against the Allied Powers of England, France, The Soviet Union, and later the United States of America

- In a short period of time, World War II spread to the corners of Europe. Very soon, it spread to European colonies in the continent of Africa

- In order to gain strategic and military advantages, the Allied Powers decided to dislodge Italy from the East African coast, where Eritrea is located, so that there would not be any Italian attacks that come from that area

- Following the Italian declaration of war on Great Britain, the British government started distributing leaflets promising Eritrean independence. Thus, war against Italy in Eritrea became inevitable. After the British declaration of war on Italy, on July 4, 1940, Italian forces began to attack Kassala, Sudan. After few hours of war, Italian forces overrun Kassala, which was under British control.

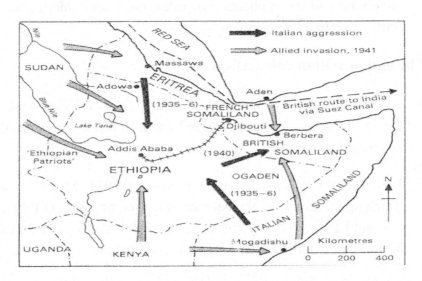

Italian invasion of Ethiopia (1935) and British attack against Italy (1941)

- In January 1941, the British forces took a counter attack against Italian forces and drove them out of Kassala. The British continued to advance to Eritrea, and from January – February of

56

1941, routed out the fleeing Italian soldiers and controlled all of western Eritrea.

- At the end, Italian forces built their defense lines at Tenqulhas, and on February 4, 6, and 10 of 1941, they thwarted British attacks.

- After this, the war stopped for a month. It was during this one month of a lull in the war that thousands of Eritrean soldier began to desert from the Italian forces and went their own ways; which could be due to the leaflets being distributed by the British promising Eritrean independence or due to the prolonged conscription or due to the two reasons.

- On March 25, 1941, British forces began to attack Italian forces at Tenqulhas. After 12 days of fighting, on 27 March, 1941, British forces occupied Keren.

- The battle at Keren was one of the fiercest battles during World War II. When the British occupied Asmara on April 1, 1941, Italian colonialism ended in Eritrea. Thus, the British set up their Administration in Eritrea.

Questions

1. What do we call the economic structure the Italians built in Eritrea?

2. How many Eritrean soldiers where in the Italian army when Italy invaded Ethiopia?

3. What was the name of the United Front that Italy joined during World War II? Which countries where part of this United Front?

Lesson 12:

Question and Discussion Period

Discussion in groups

- Every classroom forms groups, with each group electing a chairperson and secretary and discussing on assigned topics. A summary of the discussion is then presented to the class.
- Assuming a period is 60 minutes long, 25 minutes are allocated for the discussion part and the remaining 35 minutes for the group presentations.

Points for discussion (to be answered in groups):

1. The two inseparable behaviors of the military campaigns of *the royalists of Tigray were offensive attacks and amputations*. Discuss this full statement by giving examples.

2. Discuss the *reasons and outcomes of the similarities* between *Italian colonialism* in Eritrea and Emperor Menelik of Shewa's *expansion to the southern regions of the Horn of Africa*.

3. Compare and contrast Eritrean's anti-colonization resistance during the Italian *colonial period* and our armed liberation revolution.

4. 1. From the signals of 'colonial economic development' in Eritrea, what do you know? Discuss.

5. We state Eritrea was formed as a nation during Italian Colonialism. How did this happen? What was the factor that caused this?

6. The coming of Italian colonialism in Eritrea was a result of the political developments in Europe, and its end was also tied to events developed in Europe. Discuss this by explaining the end of Italian colonialism in Eritrea.

Lesson 13:

Eritrea – From Italian rule to British Administration

Lesson Goals:

At the end of this lesson, students are expected to have the following basic knowledge:

- The difference between the promises and realities of British Military Administration

- The importance of the establishment of the Association of Love of Country and the political fragmentation of the 1940s

- The trends and interferences of local and foreign powers in the future of Eritrea

British Military Administration

- Great Britain began to administer Eritrea not as a colonial power, but it was in the name of the Allied Powers. The official name of the British Administration in Eritrea was called "Administration of Occupied Enemy Territory".

- During the British Military Administration, there were no fundamental changes in the structures of the administration the Italians left. Italian officials were in charge of leadership, and there were not any changes to the laws and structures of Fascism. Thus, British Administration was a continuation European colonialism.

- In the beginning of British Administration, the Eritreans suffered a lot due to unemployment, severe food shortages, and economic crisis

- Ethnic conflicts between the Beni-Amer and Hadendewa of the Sudan continued for three years. The serves of Sahel rose up against the feudal system that oppressed them for so many years, and they called for their emancipation.

- The British Military Administration did not care or take any steps to solve the problems of the Eritrean society

- Later, when the Allied Powers needed Eritrea to use it for their war campaigns in North Africa and The Middle East, some economic improvements were registered. Exports grew; and the living standards of the society improved. This kind of economic growth continued until 1945.

The Establishment and Fragmentation of the Association for the Love of Country

- On May 5, 1941, for the first time, a modern Association was formed in Eritrea. Its name was *The Association for the Love of Country.* The Association was an important one because its goal was to speak on behalf of the rights and benefits of Eritreans, and it was anti-colonialism. Thus, it was representing Eritrean nationalism and their association.

- This Association was an important one because it was led by some prominent Eritrean political figures in the 1940s, and it led to the future political struggle. Among the prominent ones were: *Woldeab Woldemariam, Ibrahim Sultan, Abdelqadir Kebire, and Ghebremeskel Woldu. The president of the association was Ghebremeskel Woldu.*

Ghebremeskel Woldu   *Sheik Ibrahim Sultan*   *Woldeab Woldemariam*   *Abdelqadir Kebire*

- On August 3, 1944, in The Weekly Magazine, supervised by The British Administration, an editorial was published by a "certain Eritrean" that emphasized the future of Eritrea. It is rumored the writer was Brigadier Longrig, the administrator of Eritrea, which explained the potential of Eritrea and its future. However, the desire of the author was to partition Eritrea by giving the coastal areas and the highlands to Ethiopia, and the western lowlands to the Sudan.

- The editorial generated heated discussion in the weekly magazine. Some members of the Association for The Love of Country began to take the Ethiopian side. The other wing took a position for Eritrean independence and opposed union with Ethiopia. Thus, within the Association two opposing groups developed, one group called for union with Ethiopia, and the other sought independence for Eritrea.

ፃይ፡ኤርትራ፡ሰዉ፡ናዊ፡ጋዜጣ፡

THE ERITREAN WEEKLY NEWS

ASMARA - THURSDAY 2nd OCTOBER, 1947.

6th YEAR - No. 266 - PRICE: 5 CENTS E.A.

The Weekly Eritrean Newspaper: Published by The British Military Administration

In the same period and from 1943-1944, The Ethiopian government began to use certain elements of the Eritrean Coptic Tewahdo Church to work for Union with Ethiopia, and infiltrated into the Association for Love of Country

At the end of 1944, by the summons of Archbishop Markos of the Eritrean Coptic Church, those who supported union with Ethiopia, changed *The Association for Love of Country to be an Association of Union with Ethiopia*

Those who were for Eritrean independence, left the Association for Union with Ethiopia, and began to meet in secret, and worked to establish another association that would call for Eritrean independence. As a result of their meeting, they established an Association called *"Eritrea for Eritreans."* Ato Woldeab Woldemariam wrote the following piece about the establishment of the association:

*" ... first we met at Saleh Kekia's house and discussed the issues the whole day and agreed to form the New Association. We pledged to work for **Eritrea for Eritreans** without any tendencies of ethnic or regional identifications. We ate a chicken prepared by Kekia. We swore on the Quran. After that, we went to Dejazmatch Abraha's house in Mai Edaga. We ate a chicken prepared by Dejazmatch Abraha, and swore on the Bible…… ."*

- Among the founders of Eritrea for Eritreans were: *Sheik Ibrahim Sultan, Dejazmatch Hasen Ali, Dejazmatch Abraha Tesema, and others*

- The two Associations sought to get followers based on the beliefs they had for Union with Ethiopia and for Eritrean independence

- The members of *Eritrea for Eritreans* sent messengers to all corners of Eritrea and collected signatures

- Members of Union with Ethiopia also began to collect signatures and demanded immediate union with Ethiopia, and decided to present that to the British Administration

- Thus, in 1945, The Association for Love of Country splintered into two opposing groups!

The Future of Eritrea and the role of Regional and International Powers [1941-1945]

- After defeating the Italians in Eritrea, Great Britain also occupied Ethiopia and southern Somalia. Thus, the British government began to exert its influence and dominance in the eastern part of Africa.

- It is better to understand the policies of the British Administration that existed in Eritrea, especially when we consider the greater scheme it had in eastern Africa

- According to available documents from the middle of 1943, the British government had some schemes to partition Eritrea. British governors were stating that Eritreans do not have the ability to lead, and the country is too poor to be independent. These things were baseless, but were used to support the idea of partitioning Eritrea.

- The coming of the United States of America [hereafter America] into the Eritrean political scene was many before it entered World War II. Since The Allied Powers decided to use Eritrea as their military base in northeast Africa, America concluded a secret plan with the British and began its activities at the airport in Gurae.

- Soon after its activities at Gurae, in December 1941, America officially entered World War II and the number of military experts and soldiers in Eritrea grew, and there were about 1,000 of them.

- As it was stated in a previous lesson, after the defeat of Italy in Eritrea, the British began to administer Ethiopia. Rather than being controlled by the British, Emperor Haile Sellasie of Ethiopia decided to ally himself with the Americans.

- At this time, Ethiopia and America signed an agreement of cooperation. Hence, the influence of the British in Ethiopia began to decline. The British government officially accepted the Ogaden region to be part of Ethiopia, [unofficially, some territories of the Ogaden were under British control].

- In several occasions, Ethiopia began to present to the British and Americans about its desire to control Eritrea.

- In the coming lessons, we will continue to explain the key role America and Ethiopia played in deciding the future of Eritrea.

Questions

1. In a few years, when the British controlled Eritrea, what was the reason that made the Eritrean economy grow?

2. Mention some key nationalist figures who were the founders of the Eritrea for Eritreans.

3. How did the influence of America begin in Eritrea and the region?

Lesson 14:

The end of World War II - Internal conditions of Eritrea and its Future

---

Lesson Goals:

At the end of this lesson, students are expected to have the following basic knowledge:

- Reasons for the socio-economic crisis, banditry, and unrest in Eritrea
- Goals and outcomes of the meeting at Biet Gergish [Waala Biet Gergish]
- General tendencies and conditions of the political associations in Eritrea
- The establishment and positions of different political associations in Eritrea

---

Socio-economic condition, banditry, and unrest in Eritrea

- When World War II ended in 1945, the unitary and economic condition of Eritrea began to decline. It was at this time that the British Administration started to dismantle the economic infrastructures of Eritrea that were built by the Italians and those that were built during World War II.

- In general, in the port city of Massawa, port and docking facilities were sold and removed, and overall, 75 buildings were demolished. Airport facilities that were in Gurae, Assab, and Zula were dismantled or met the same fate of those in Massawa!

- In addition to what was stated above, Cable Lines, cement factory tools, and other infrastructures were dismantled, removed, and sold. Hence, the living conditions of Eritreans began to go from bad to worse; unemployment and lack of farming areas compounded the economic crisis.

Buildings Destroyed by the British Administration

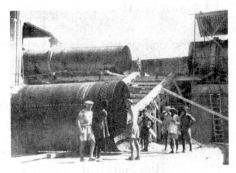

A Cement Factory sold by the British Administration

- The Ethiopian government, through its representative in Asmara, *Colonel Nega Haile Sellasie,* began to use The Association of Union with Ethiopia and the Youth wing of the Union as tools, and unleashed banditry and unrest in Eritrea.

- In 1945-46, the Unionist Group began to take brutal and antagonistic steps. Anti-foreigner sentiments, especially anti-Italians and Arabs, reached at the top. In March 1946, supporters of the Unionists staged a fight in Keren and Massawa.

- In August 1946, the unrest that was staged by the Unionists showed its ugly face in Asmara. The unrest killed 46 citizens and wounded 70 others, which was led by Sudanese soldiers under the control the British Administration. Ethiopia and the Unionists sought to equate this incident as a religious conflict. The British Administration took this incident as an opportune way to continue with its partition plan, and did not take any steps to investigate or calm the unrest.

The Waala [Meeting] of Biet Gergish

- Under the circumstances mentioned above, Woldeab Woldemariam of Eritrea for Eritreans, and Gheberemskel Woldu of Union with Ethiopia called a meeting of reconciliation to save Eritrea from being partitioned. The meeting took place at Biet Gergish on November 24, 1946.

- Due to the intrigues played by colonel Nega and his followers, who were members of the Unionist Group, the meeting disbanded without any resolution. Hence, the Ethiopian government replaced Ghebremeskel Woldu, who had a spirit of reconciliation and a middle of the road position, by a diehard Unionist called *Tedla Bairu*.

- The Unionist Association confirmed its position as the tool of the Ethiopian government. The debacle of the meeting of Biet Gergish clearly revealed the nationalist nature of the Eritrean political landscape. When time came to form political parties, the choice and tendencies of being on the side of Union with Ethiopia or having and Independent Eritrea became clearer.

Political Associations in Eritrea

- The British Administration allowed the rights of political activities in Eritrea in the middle of 1940s. Right after the failure of Waala Biet Gergish, and before the coming of the Commission of Inquiry of the Four Powerful countries, many Eritrean politicians who had different political tendencies, began to move, hold meetings, and to form their political associations.

- In general and at this junction, the political organizations of Eritreans lacked consciousness and power; and were at their rudimentary and beginning stages. Therefore, the Associations or later called parties had weak organizational level!

- Using a common terminology, we may call the associations of the 1940s as political parties, but they were proto-parties, and did not have developed real organization, organizational structure, popular support, and clear political programs. Continuous division and changing of membership were their hallmarks.

- Based on their political tendencies, these associations *can be divided into two groups*: those who supported Union with Ethiopia and those who wanted to have an Independent Eritrea. The list of the parties and their goals were:

1. *Moslem League*

- This was established in Keen on December 7, 1946; and its *main founder was Ibrahim Sultan.* In its first meeting in Keren, *it elected Said Bekri Almirqani as president, and Ibrahim Sultan as its general-secretary*. The League was calling for an immediate Eritrean independence, especially when the British left. It had an official newspaper called *Sewet*, published in Arabic.

2. *Unionist Association*

- Even though it existed earlier, it was on January 1, 1947, that it officially was established in Asmara. *It elected Dejazmatch Beyene Beraki as its president, and Tedla Bairu as its general-secretary.* Its main objective was Union with Ethiopia.

It had an official newspaper called *"Ethiopia"*, published in Tigrigna.

3. Eritrea for Eritreans [Liberal Progressive Party]

- This was founded in Adi Qeyh in February 1947, and *had Ra'si Tesema Asmerom as its president, and Dejazmatch Measho Zeweldi as its general-secretary.* This Association called for Eritrean independence after 10 years of British care-taker government.

4. Pro-Italy Party

- This party was established in July 1947, and *Idris Hasen was its president, while Mahanzel Tesfazgy was its secretary.* Its objective was Eritrean independence after 15 years of Italian care-taker government. It had a newspaper called *"Berhan Eritrea"*, published in Tigrigna.

- In addition to this party, there were smaller associations, such as Free Association, Islamic National Party, and Italo-Eritrean Association.

- The different groups mentioned above, using their newspapers, political discussions, and debates were able to promote the development of Eritrean political consciousness

The *"Sewet" Newspaper*

The *"Ethiopia" newspaper*

Questions

1. After the end of World War II, what was the cause for the decline of Eritrean economy?

2. Who were the organizers of The Waala [Meeting] Biet Gergish? What was the main objective of the Waala?

3. What was the main cause for the abandonment of the meeting?

4. Explain the main characteristics of the Eritrean political Associations of the 1940s.

Lesson 15:

Eritrea – from the hands of Allied Powers to the United Nations

---

Lesson Goals:

At the end of this lesson, students are expected to have the following basic knowledge:

- The different views and reasons of the Allied Powers on the future of Eritrea

- The transfer of the Eritrean case to the United Nations [hereafter, UN]

- The contents and plan of "Bevin-Sforza"

- The response of Eritrean political parties to the Bevin-Sforza plan

---

The Allied Powers and the future of Eritrea

- World War II ended by the victory of the Allied Powers. The victors began to discuss the future of Eritrea and other Italian colonies, such as Libya and Somalia.

- Due to the opposing views and interests they had, The Allied Powers could not agree on the future of Eritrea. Hence, they set up an Inquiry Commission chosen from each country, and sent it to Eritrea. From the end of 1947 and the beginning of 1948, the

Inquiry Commission met with the representatives of the Eritrea society.

- The visit coincided with the unrest and banditry organized by Ethiopia and members of the Unionist Group. The organized political unrest and banditry targeted those who were in favor of Eritrean independence. The assassination attempts carried on Ato Woldeab Woldemariam on July 6, 1947, and the one against Dejazmatch Hasen Ali carried out on July 9, 1947, can be cited as examples of terror. Therefore, the visit of the Inquiry Commission was a time of terror in Eritrea.

- Between November 12, 1947 and January 3, 1948, the Inquiry Commission met with the representatives of the Eritrean society and other members of the community. Instead of forming a united front, the organizations that were in favor of Eritrean independence met with the Inquiry Commission separately and presented their petitions.

- The Unionist party presented its petition for a complete union with Ethiopia, and those that were for Eritrean independence submitted various petitions that would call for independence.

- In its final report, the Commission stated the number of Eritreans seeking independence was greater than those who sought union with Ethiopia.

- The Eritrean case, in addition to the other Italian colonies' issues, became a complicated issue and was difficult to get a solution.

- On September 15, 1948, The Allied Powers met in Paris, but did not come up with a solution. Therefore, the Eritrean case was transferred to the UN.

The Eritrean Case at the General Assembly of the UN

- Since The Allied Powers could not agree on a solution, the case of former Italian colonies, Eritrea, Libya, and Somalia, was transferred to the United Nations, but it was not free of complications

- In April 1949, representatives of the Eritrean political parties planned to go to Lake Success, US, to present their case to the United Nations. Before their departure, one of the founders of the Moslem League, Abdelqadir Kebire, was assassinated in Asmara by agents of the Ethiopian government.

- At the 3rd UN meeting at Lake Success, Ibrahim Sultan of the Moslem League, Blata Mahmud Abdela of Pro-Italy, Tedla Bairu of the Unionists, Cacianni of Italo-Eritrea, and other Eritreans were present.

- The Eritrean representatives presented their petitions to The UN.

The Bevin-Sforza Plan

- When the case of former Italian colonies, Eritrea, Libya, and Somalia was transferred to the UN, the influence of Italy began to grow.

- While the debates on the former colonies cases' at the UN were continuing, the Italian foreign minister Carlo Sforza, and his British counter-part, Ernest Bevin, began to discuss and agreed on a plan. The two agreed for independence on some parts about Libya and Somalia, but decided to partition Eritrea, the western lowlands to go to the Sudan, and the rest to be given to Ethiopia.

73

- When the Bevin-Sforza plan was presented to the UN, it was narrowly defeated. This plan of partition angered the Eritrean people.

- The Eritreans who were at Lake Success, especially those who were for Independence, showed a united front and opposed the plan. Since the plan was at the point of being adopted, it gave the pro-independence parties a lesson to think of, and helped them unite.

- In September 1949, at its Fourth Session, the UN decided on the fate of Libya and Somalia, but did not find a solution to the Eritrean case. Hence, the UN set up a Commission of Inquiry composed of Five countries to find the "wishes of the Eritrean people", and decided to send it to Eritrea.

Questions

1. What was the reason the Eritrean case was referred to the UN?

2. What was the Bevin-Sforza plan?

3. Explain the direct impact of the Bevin-Sforza plan on the Eritrean political scene

Lesson 16:

The Establishment of the Independence Block and the coming of the United Nations Commission of Enquiry [hereafter, UNCE] to Eritrea

---

Lesson Goals:

At the end of this lesson, students are expected to have the following basic knowledge:

- The reasons and importance of the establishment of the Independence Block and the reaction of the Unionist Association

- The activities of the UNCE and causes of the unrest of that time

- Causes for the division within the Independence Block

The Establishment of the Independence Block

- In our previous lesson, we pointed out that those Eritreans who were pro-Independence and who attended the UN meeting at Lake Success had formed a united front. When they returned to Eritrea, in January 1950, they met in Dekemhare and formed the Independence Block that included several parties and demanded Eritrean independence. A decision was made to have "Hanti Ertra [One Eritrea] as the official newspaper of the party.

- At the 2nd meeting of the party, and during an election process, the party elected Ras Tesema Asmerom as president, and Ibrahim Sultan as general-secretary.

- The British government estimated the Independence Block represented 75% of the Eritrean people. Many who were members

75

of the Unionist Party formed "Free Eritrea Party" and joined with the Independence Block.

Ras Tesema Asmerom

Hanti Ertra [One Eritrea]: the official newspaper of the Independence Block

- Members of the Unionist Association, who thought the Independence Block can't be stopped, decided to unleash a condition of terror and banditry in Eritrea. The Eritrean Orthodox Church, under the leadership of Archbishop Markos, began to impose spiritual intimidation on the members and decided to excommunicate those who favored independence, and who were nationalists.

- On February 3, 1950, there was a 3rd attempt to assassinate Ato Woldeab Woldemariam. Previously, in 1947, there were two attempts to assassinate him. Overall, there were seven attempts to kill Ato Woldeab Woldemariam.

The Coming of the UNCI to Eritrea

- When the UN Commission came to Eritrea on February 8, 1950, it found unrest in all corners of the land. The worst unrest was the one that took place in Asmara on February 12, 1950.

- At that time, the Commission was in Eritrea for only two weeks. The unrest that continued until February 27, and which had the tendency of religious conflict, caused tens of Eritreans to die, and destroyed several infrastructures and homes.

- Nevertheless, Eritrean elders and leaders took a personal initiative, called for reconciliation, and calmed the unrest. On the opposite side, the British Administration did not take any steps to resolve the unrest. For its own political interest, the British Administration attempted to use the unrest to plan for the partition of Eritrea.

- It is confirmed through some sources, the unrest was instigated by the British Administration, because it did not try to solve the problem before it started or after it ended. It is within this context and experience that the Eritrean people must consider the British Administration as conniving and divisive.

- All of the unrest took place while the Commission, composed of Burma, Pakistan, Norway, Guatemala, and South Africa, was in Eritrea and conducting its work

The Division within the Independence Block

- British Administrators who knew the strength of the Independence Block thought it was going to weaken their plan of partition, and decided to infiltrate and dismantle the smaller parties within the Independence Block

- The "divide-and-rule" tactics of the British was well known all over the world. Hence, British Administrators began to practice the same evil tactic in Eritrea

- The British Administrator of Eritrea at that time, G.K.N. Trevaskis, summoned the leaders of Tigre notables and told them that they would lose power, and duped them to form a new Moslem League. Thus, Sheik Ali Reday became the president of the new party and demanded a separate independence for the western lowlands of Eritrea.

- Another British intelligence officer, Brigadier Stafford, convinced Dejazmatch Abraha Tesema and his followers to withdraw from the Eritrea for Eritreans [Progressive Liberal party] and form a new party called "Free Union with Ethiopia". Hence, the new demand was "Union with Agreement". Using the above mentioned intrigues, the British Administration scored some victory in dismantling the Independence Block.

Questions

1. What was the clear reason to the establishment of the Independence Block?
2. According to the 1949 estimate of the UN CE what was the percentage of Eritreans that supported independence?
3. Which countries were members of the UN CE to Eritrea?
4. Describe briefly the reasons for the division within the Independence Block

Lesson 17:

The Decision of the General Assembly of the UN

Lesson Goals:

At the end of this lesson, students are expected to have the following basic knowledge:

- Conclusions and different views of the member countries of the UNCE
- The connection between the interests of America and the decision of the Federal Arrangement of 3090(A)V

The Report of the UNCE

- When the Commission finished its report, it came to three opposing conclusions. Pakistan and Guatemala proposed independence. Burma and South Africa proposed Federation with Ethiopia. Norway proposed that the Highlands, Semhar, and the Dankalia to be united with Ethiopia, and the lowlands should remain under British control, but later, by a plebiscite, be joined with the Sudan or Ethiopia.

- In September 1950, the Eritrean case was submitted to the General Assembly of the UN. The General Assembly chose a temporary committee to study the case. The representatives of Eritrea were invited to submit their views. The Soviet Union proposed independence, but Great Britain and America rejected it.

- America proposed Eritrea be federated with Ethiopia under the protection of the Ethiopian crown. Ibrahim Sultan and Woldeab

Woldemariam who represented the Independence Block rejected the American proposal. Both submitted strong warning by stating Eritreans do not allow their country to be wiped out of the world map, and will not be yoked with their old enemy, Ethiopia. They called for an absolute Eritrean independence.

- Ibrahim Sultan gave the following prophetic words at the UN:

"Even from ancient times, Eritrea was never under the control of Ethiopia. …. Did not the popular uprising start against them [the Ethiopians] so that the country [Eritrea] would not be under their control? If you comprehend the evidences submitted, are you contemplating to join Eritrea in a Federation with the historical enemy? … Why are we being denied the same natural right of nations to be independent? Why are we being denied the same rights bestowed upon Libya and Somalia? If a wrong decision is going to be taken, for all of the forced steps we take to oppose the decision, fight for our rights, gain our freedom, safe guard our survival, the members of this committee will be responsible for any unrest or turmoil that erupts in east Africa".

The Decision of the General Assembly of the UN: 390(A) V

- On December 2, 1950, the General Assembly of the UN adopted the Federal Arrangement that was proposed by America and its followers

- Based on what was submitted, 46 countries voted for the Federation and 10 opposed it.

- The decision stated Eritrea will have its domestic independence and internal government, but would be united with Ethiopia through a Federal Arrangement.

- A Federal Arrangement usually takes place between two or more equal countries, and it is done through a free-will decision of the parties. The countries that accept the Federal Arrangement set up a common foreign, defense, economic, and other structures that would enhance their common goals. They administer their internal affairs. In the Eritrean case, the opposite plan was decided. It was not decided that Eritrea be an independent and free country, but to be yoked under the Ethiopian crown, which was a deformed type of arrangement.

- After the decision, on December 1951, a Peace Conference was organized in Asmara. All party and religious leaders met and called for reconciliation.

- Before the implementation of the Federal Arrangement, a Commissioner was appointed to go to Eritrea to draft a constitution, and set up the first election for the Eritrean Assembly. It was also decided that the Federal Arrangement would be implemented when the Eritrean Assembly accepts the constitution, and when the Ethiopian Emperor approves it.

- From all of the political parties that were in Eritrea, no one accepted the Federal Arrangement, except the smaller party that was called "Free Moslem League". From the beginning, the Federal Decision was set up to safe guard American interests, and its ally Ethiopia.

- According to revealed secret documents, the then American Secretary of State, Foster Dulles, stated the Federal Arrangement was planned to maintain American interests by ignoring Eritrean justice.

John Foster Dulles wrote the following: "from the point of view of justice, the opinions of the Eritrean people must receive consideration. Nevertheless, the strategic interest of the United States in the Red Sea basin and considerations of security and world peace make it necessary that the country [Eritrea] has to be linked with our ally, Ethiopia."

Questions

1. Mention the countries of the UNCE that proposed Eritrean Independence
2. Which country proposed a Federal Arrangement?
3. Explain why America wanted Eritrea to be united with Ethiopia.

Lesson 18:

Discussion in groups

- Every classroom forms groups, with each group electing a chairperson and secretary and discussing on assigned topics. A summary of the discussion is then presented to the class.
- Assuming a period is 60 minutes long, 25 minutes are allocated for the discussion part and the remaining 35 minutes for the group presentations.

Points for discussion (to be answered in groups):

1. The British presented a plan to partition Eritrea because of Eritrea's inability to be economically self-sufficient. In principle, can a state of being self–sufficient or not, be a measuring yard to the existence of independent nations? Discuss this concept.

2. The Waala of Biet Gergish was able to identify the nature of Eritrean politics of the 1940s. In what way did this happen?

3. At the UN, the Eritreans were represented by various political parties that had different views. How did these views affect the question of Eritrean independence?

4. The concept of "divide –and-rule" was a general phenomenon, and the British tactic was a peculiar one. Discuss the meaning and consequence of this concept.

5. Discuss the Federation that was decided between Eritrea and Ethiopia, which makes it different from the other types of federations.

Lesson 19:

The Stage for the Federal Arrangement and the Establishment of the Eritrean Government

---

Lesson Goals:

At the end of this lesson, students are expected to have the following basic knowledge:

- The Mission and work of Anze Matienzo
- The process of electing the Eritrean Assembly, the adoption of the Eritrean constitution, and structure of the Eritrean Government
- Then process of transferring power to the Eritrean and Ethiopian Governments

---

Commissioner Anze Matienzo in Eritrea

- Anze Matienzo, a Bolivian diplomat, was chosen according to the decision of 390(A) V, and was sent to Eritrea. His mission was to draft an Eritrean constitution, supervise the election of the Eritrean assembly, establish the Eritrean government, and implement the provisions of the Federal Arrangement

- When Matienzo arrived in Eritrea, he found unrest and turmoil. He emphasized that he can't continue his work while the unrest and turmoil are going on. Hence, in August 1951, the British Administration declared amnesty to all *shefatu* [bandits who were causing the unrest and turmoil]. About 90% of the bandits surrendered. Nevertheless, the acts of terrorism did not stop!

84

- The Independence Block Party changed its name to Democratic Party of Eritrea and stated it will fight for internal independence of Eritrea and the provisions of the Federal Arrangement

The Eritrean Assembly and Constitution

- Under 300(A)V, it was stipulated that an Eritrean Assembly must ratify the constitution drafted by Matienzo. Hence, an election was conducted in Eritrea. After a direct and by representation process, 68-member Assembly was elected. It was only in Asmara and Massawa that direct voting took place. Even in those places, only men were elected. There were no women! In other place of Eritrea, voting was done through representatives of the people, such as elders, leaders, and notables of the areas who served as an electoral college.

- Out of the 68 members of the Assembly, 32 were Unionists, 21 Democratic Party members, and 15 were of the Moslem League of Western Lowlands. Thus, the Unionists and the Moslem League created a coalition and obtained a majority vote in the Assembly. The two groups took a favorable Ethiopian side in the Assembly, which helped in the debates and drafting of the Eritrean constitution.

- In the debate that considered the existence of Eritrea and the Eritrean flag, the coalition group wanted to have only an Ethiopian flag. The Democratic Party called for the existence of the Eritrean Assembly and to have a flag. They won!

- There was no solution to the debate about an official language and the post of a representative of the Ethiopian crown. The debate in the Assembly became heated. The Unionists debated to make Amharic an official language, and to have a representative of the crown. The Democratic Party debated to have Tigrigna and Arabic

85

as the official languages, and rejected the need of a representative of the Ethiopian crown in Eritrea.

- Ethiopia stated the Executive Branch of the Eritrea government must be chosen by the Ethiopian Emperor. The idea was rejected by the Assembly.

- At the end of the debate, it was decided to have Tigrigna and Arabic as the official languages, and to have a representative of the crown in Eritrea. However, it was also decided that the role and responsibilities of the representative would be limited.

- In its general scope, the Eritrean constitution had 99 articles, which had the guarantees of human rights, the division of the branches of government, and importance of the rule of law.

- The Eritrean constitution was contrary to the feudal Ethiopian constitution. To give n example, let us compare the 1955 revised constitution of Ethiopia, and articles 17/18 of the Eritrean constitution.

- The Ethiopian version in article 4 states: "due to his lineage from the Solomonic Dynasty, and being chosen by God, the Emperor is a holy man. His honor is not to be violated, his power is not questionable ... He who attempts to hurt the emperor will be punished."
- The Eritrean versions of articles 17/18 state: "The Eritrean constitution is based on the democratic principle of a government. ... All government officials are elected from within the general public. ... They are elected through free and fair voting process. They work to serve the people."

The Transfer of Power to the Governments of Eritrea and Ethiopia

- When the structure of the Eritrean government reached its final form, the Ethiopian government, in the name of the Federal Government, took responsibilities over most Eritrean government properties, infrastructures, transportation, and offices.
- As an excuse to defend the Eritrean borders, "The Ethiopian Army" built barracks in Asmara, Massawa, Assab, and other places.
- On September 11, 1952, when the Ethiopian Emperor ratified the Eritrean constitution, it was on September 15, 1952, that the Union Jack [British flag] came down, and the Eritrean and Ethiopian flags replacedit.

Anze Matienzo with members of the Eritrea Assembly

Emperor Haile Sellasie Crossing the Mereb River

Questions

1. What was the main reason the British Administration declared amnesty to the bandits?
2. What was the new name of the Independence Block? Why did it change its name?
3. There was a direct and indirect election in Eritrea. Explain the difference between direct and indirect election.

Lesson 20:

The First Years of the Eritrean Government

Lesson Goals:
At the end of this lesson, students are expected to have the following basic knowledge:

- Economic Crisis and its consequences
- Methods used by the Ethiopian Government to violate Eritrean Democratic Rights
- The Role and Importance of the Free Trade Association of Eritrean Workers

As stipulated, the Constitutional Assembly should have been dissolved, and new one should been elected, especially after the ratification of the Eritrean Constitution. Since that was not done, the Assembly continued. From within the Assembly, an Executive Branch was elected. Tedla Bairu became the Chief Executive of The Eritrean Government. Ali Reday became the Chairman of the Assembly, and Blata Demsas Woldemichael was elected as the Vice Chairman. Bitweded Endargachew Messay, son-in-law of Emperor Haile Sellasie, became the Representative of the Ethiopian Crown.

Tedla Bairu, Head of the Eritrean Government (1952-1955)

Economic Crisis

- Since the important economic centers were transferred to Ethiopia, mainly in the name of the Federal Government, the Eritrean Government was deprived of revenue resources

- To illustrate this, we give the following examples that were transferred to Ethiopia: income from the Sea ports, taxation, finance, and external trade. These were sources of revenue for Eritrea. The railway lines and road transportation were also transferred to Ethiopia. Hence, Eritrea was left without any source of revenue!

- Due to the weak economy, factories began to close, and the economic activity started to decline. In the cities, unemployment increased, and the living conditions of the people deteriorated

- Within a month of the Eritrean Government's existence, workers began to demonstrate, mainly due to economic hardships. In order to alleviate the economic condition of the country and improve wages, the workers demanded a solution to the high prices of the markets, and the harsh condition of the citizens. Nevertheless, there was not any improvement!

The Violation of Eritrean Democratic Rights

- According to the Federal Arrangement of the UN, an equal number of elected Eritrean and Ethiopian officials were to from a Federal Assembly. The elected Eritrean officials went to Addis Ababa, the Ethiopian capital, but they returned home without doing anything, and without being recognized!

- *"One Eritrea",* an official newspaper of the Independence Block, changed its name during the Federation, and became The *Voice of*

Eritrea. Through its editors, Mohamed Saleh Mahmud and Elias Teklu, The Voice of Eritrea was expressing the economic hardships of the people, and it was also defending the domestic independence of Eritrea.

The Voice of Eritrea Newspaper

Mohamed Saleh Mahmud   *Elias Teklu*

- Ethiopian authorities who could not tolerate the individual rights of freedom of express began to investigate the editors of The Voice of Eritrea. These authorities accused the editors and took them to court. Hence, the Newspaper was shut down for a year!

- After one year, in 1954, it began its publication. Again, the Ethiopian authorities filed suit against the Newspaper, and the case was transferred to the Federal Court [it was an Ethiopian court]. At that time, the Newspaper was shut down for good! Its editors were sentenced from 3-8 years, and were taken to prison in Adi Quala.

- The Ethiopian government declared the Supreme Court of Ethiopia was to be The Court of the Federation, with its final decision making power, and usurped the authority of the Eritrean Supreme Court

- All of the steps taken by the Ethiopian government were against the provisions of the UN Federal Arrangement. Using these tactics, the democratic rights of the Eritrean people were violated!

Free Trade Association of Eritrean Workers

- Eritrean workers have been fighting for their rights. In 1952, at the end of its rule, the British Administration issued a proclamation that would allow workers to get organized into Trade Unions.

- When the Free Trade Union of Eritrean Workers adopted its constitution, in November 1952, it conducted its election. *It elected Ato Woldeab as its president, and Siraj Abdu as the Vice President.*

- In the beginning of the Federation, the Trade Union was an advocate of internal Eritrean independence, and an opponent of Ethiopian hegemony. Due to this position, Ethiopian authorities began to dismantle the Trade Union.

- There were seven assassination attempts on Ato Woldeab Woldemariam. After he recuperated, he was forced to go into exile to live in Egypt.

- Ethiopian authorities continued to control the Trade Union, and prevented it from conducting its activities

Questions

1. Mention the main Eritrean economic sectors that were taken over by the Ethiopian government during the Federation

2. List the demands of the Eritrean Trade Union when it went on a strike

3. What was the main reason The Voice of Eritrea was banned?

Lesson 21:

The Opposition of the Eritrean People to the gradual dismantling of the federal arrangement

---

Lesson Goals:

At the end of this lesson, students are expected to have the following basic knowledge:

- Opposition within the Eritrean Assembly and the factors that led to the downfall of Tedla Bairu's Administration

- The beginning of the Students' Movement

- The Workers' Strike of 1958, its causes, and results

Opposition within the Eritrean Assembly

- When the Eritrean economic crisis became worse, and as Ethiopian interference grew stronger, members of the Eritrean Assembly began to express their opposition. The open opposition was not only raised by Ibrahim Sultan, Omer Hakito, Dejzamatch Ghebrezgy Guangul, but it also was raised by some members of the Unionist Party, such as Aba Habtemariam Negru, Embaye Ghebreamlack, and others.

- As the Ethiopian interference increased, on February 13, 1954, 29 members of the Eritrean Assembly asked Tedla Bairu to call an emergency meeting. The Chief Executive refused! Due to his

93

refusal, and other reasons, the relationship between Tedla and the Assembly became sour.

- In addition to their opposition, members of the Assembly were sending messages to the UN Representative, the consulates of the USA, Great Britain, France, Italy, and the Sudan about the dismantling of the Federation by Ethiopia

- In similar developments, in the election of 1953, Ato Woldeab won a seat in the Assembly, but was barred by Tedla. That was one phase of what Tedla was doing to violate the democratic rights of citizens.

The Downfall of Tedla Bairu's Administration

- Tedla Bairu did not only antagonize members of the Assembly, including those of the Unionist Party; he also created a rift with the Imperial Crown Representative, Endargachew Messay. Endargachew plotted a plan and began to work with an ultra-Unionist Eritrean Priest, Qeshi Dimetrios Ghebremariam, to topple Tedla Bairu.

- In 1955, some members of the Eritrean Assembly who were anti-Tedla, being led by Qeshi Dimetrios, went to Addis Ababa and submitted petitions to the Emperor to remove Tedla. The main accusations were the amnesty he gave to the bandits, and his authoritarian administration. Emperor Haile Sellasie summoned Tedla to Addis Ababa, and ordered him to resign, because he made members of the Assembly angry.

- As a result of the order, on July 18, 1955, Tedla Bairu resigned as Chief Executive of the Eritrean Government! After a few days, Ali Reday also resigned. Tedla's position was taken by Asfeha Woldemichael, who was Endargachew's Deputy. In an election that took place at the Assembly, Idris Mohamed Adem became its president.

- In 1956, during the Second election of the Assembly, by the intriguing plots devised by Asfeha, Qeshi Dimetrios, and the Chief of Police, colonel Tedla Ogbit [later became general], the Eritrean Assembly was dominated by Unionists.

The Movement of Students and Workers

- In May 1957, students at Haile Sellasie 1st High School, demonstrated against the introduction of Amharic language in the school, and they demanded the respect of the people's rights. The students were influenced by the radio broadcasts of At Woldeab from Cairo.

- After a few days, students from other schools in Asmara and Eritrean cities followed the same steps taken by those at Haile Sellasie 1st, and demonstrated against the steps being taken by the Ethiopian government. As a result, many students were arrested!

- On March 10, 1958, workers went on strike against the new labor law. In Asmara, about 20,000 people took part in the demonstration. In the demonstration that took three days, there were some unrest and shootings. The police killed tens of workers, and about 80 workers and the Labor Union leaders were arrested.

- When police brutality continued unabated, the Labor Union leaders advised the workers to return to work. The situation became calm. After a few months, The Labor Union was disbanded. It needs to be recalled, similar Labor Union strikes also took place in Assab and Massawa.

- The Students' and Workers' Movements, which surpassed the ethnic, religious, and sub-nationalist tendencies of the 1940s, gave birth to the newly coordinated, modern, national, social, political, and conscious Eritrean movement. That was an important and a positive step in the development of Eritrean national identity. Therefore, the Eritrean Liberation Movement [Harakat in Arabic, or Mahber Shewate, Group of Seven], that started in 1958, was the outcome of the Students' and Workers' Movements.

Questions

1. List the names of members of the Eritrean Assembly who were opposing the interference of the Ethiopian government

2. List the names of countries that the members of the Eritrean Assembly sent petitions.

3. List in a consecutive order the people who replaced Tedla Bairu and Ali Reday in 1955 as The Chief Executive of the Eritrean Government, and president of the Eritrean Assembly.

Lesson 22:

The Establishment of Eritrean Liberation Movement (ELM) [Haraka, in Arabic]

Lesson Goals:

At the end of this lesson, students are expected to have the following basic knowledge:

- The beginning and organization of ELM
- The Weaknesses of ELM

The Establishment of ELM

The First cell of ELM started on November 2, 1958, in Port Sudan. Among the founders were: Mohamed Said Nawud, Mohamed Al Hasen Osman, Osman Mohamed Osman, and Ahmed Eyay.

Mohamed Said Nawud

97

- The reason why ELM started in The Sudan was because of the police surveillance in Eritrea in the 1950s, and thus it was difficult to start such a movement inside Eritrea, The main goals of ELM were:

   1. Ensure and preserve the unity of the Eritrean people
   2. Usher Eritrean independence
   3. Establish democratic institutions

- In 1959, ELM started to take some form of organization in Eritrea. Saleh Eyay was assigned to organize members in Keren and the Barka region. Yasin Aqda was assigned to organize in the Highlands and Semhar areas. The organizational structure of ELM was very secretive. ELM's Executive Staff was stationed in Port Sudan. *The cells were organized in a Group of Seven people who operated inside and outside of Eritrea.* A Group was not allowed to know another person outside of its own Group! Each member had sworn to dedicate himself to the national cause. In such way, ELM was able to organize many citizens inside Eritrea. Each Group [Cell] was conducting meeting to discuss national issues. Such an organization played a major role in the development of the nationalist consciousness of the members of a cell.

Weaknesses of ELM

- There was no solid communication between the Executive Staff in The Sudan and members of the Cells inside Eritrea. Hence, ELM failed to capitalize on the ripe situation that would have helped in starting of the Armed Struggle against the Ethiopian Empire.

- ELM's plan of overthrowing the Ethiopian government by force, and declaring independence did not take into account the objective realities of Eritrea and The Federation.

- On September 1, 1961, when Idris Hamid Awate, in the name of Eritrean Liberation Front [hereafter, ELF], declared the war of independence, many members of ELM joined him. Hence, ELM's political influence began to decline. Nevertheless, it should not be forgotten that ELM had a major influence in the development of Eritrean nationalism and the political consciousness of the citizens.

Questions

1. Why did ELM start its activities outside of Eritrea?
2. Mention the nationals who were recruiting ELM members inside Eritrea
3. List the major weaknesses of ELM

Lesson 23:

The End of the Federal Arrangement and the Official Annexation of Eritrea by Ethiopia

---

Lesson Goals:

At the end of this lesson, students are expected to have the following basic knowledge:

1. Preparation to dissolve the Federation
2. Opposition of Eritreans against the Ethiopian steps
3. Declaration of Annexation of Eritrea by Ethiopia

Preparations to Dissolve the Federation

In November 1958, the Ethiopian government replaced the Eritrean flag by an Ethiopian flag. This step became the beginning of the end of the inevitable. After some time, in May 1960, the name Eritrean Government was replaced by "Eritrean Administration". The Eritrean seal was replaced by an Ethiopian seal!

In addition to what has been done, by September 1960, the Ethiopian Government put all Eritrean schools under its control. Amharic replaced Tigrigna and Arabic, and it became the official langue in Eritrea. These actions were contrary to the UN Federal Arrangement!

Opposition to the steps taken by the Ethiopian Government

- The steps taken to dissolve the Federation caused some uproar among Eritreans. Students opposed the control of Eritrean schools by the Ethiopian government. As a result, 36 Eritrean students were detained for four months.

- As mentioned in a previous lesson, in September 1, 1961, the ELF had started by Hamid Idris Awate. In 1962, the ELF attacked Akurdet, and 3 government officials were killed, plus 62 civilians were wounded.

- In 1962, members of the ELF that included Ghebremdhin and his colleagues, tried to assassinate Qeshi Dimetrios. Ghebremedhin was wounded. This heroic Eritrean, while he was in the hospital, instead of revealing any secrets, he committed suicide. It was in such ways that Eritreans were expressing their anger against the creeping dissolution of the Federation.

Annexation of Eritrea by Ethiopia

The impending annexation was clear to everyone. On November 13, 1962, the Ethiopian government ordered all police forces to leave their posts and go home. Asmara fell under the control of "The Ethiopian Army [called Tor Serawit]". The army marched in the streets of Asmara shouting *"give a bullet to the one who disobeys"*. Ethiopian jet fighters flew over Asmara all day and created fear in the minds of the citizens!

The next day, on November 14, 1962, The Eritrean Assembly was surrounded by the Ethiopian Army. Asfeha entered the Assembly Hall being escorted by Tedla Ogbit. Asfeha spoke in Amharic and declared Eritrea has become part of Ethiopia, and the Federation was dissolved! Before asking members of the Assembly to accept his declaration, he thanked them for their approval. That was the way how the Federation was dissolved, and how Eritrea was annexed completely and became a part of Ethiopia.

To oppose the annexation, leaders of ELF in Asmara staged a mass demonstration. However, the demonstration was disbanded by the police force. Many leaders and *members of the ELF in Asmara that included: Mahmud Ismail, Saleh Eyay, Musa Afho, Tekue Yihdego, Kahsay Bahlebi, Woldenkiel Abraha, and Teklay Ghebreselassie were arrested.* During this time, the Eritrean people have already carried out an armed struggle against the Ethiopian government to usher Eritrean independence.

Questions

1. Describe the reasons why the "Eritrean Government" was changed to "Eritrean Administration, the Eritrean flag was replaced by an Ethiopia, and give the month and year of the change.
2. How did Eritreans express their outage about the dissolution of the Federation?
3. When and how did the Federation get dissolved?

Lesson 24:

Question and Discussion Period

Discussion in groups

- Every classroom forms groups, with each group electing a chairperson and secretary and discussing on assigned topics. A summary of the discussion is then presented to the class.
- Assuming a period is 60 minutes long, 25 minutes are allocated for the discussion part and the remaining 35 minutes for the group presentations.

Points for discussion (to be answered in groups):

1. During the Federation, Eritrea had its official languages, flag, Assembly, and government. Discuss the influence of these symbols in the development of Eritrean nationalism and identity.
2. The Eritrean constitution was democratic, while the Ethiopian constitution was feudal and absolute/authoritarian. Discuss the problems that would come when countries that have stark differences are yoked together in a Federal Arrangement.
3. Discuss role the Eritrean Trade Union played in fostering Eritrean identity and political struggle
4. Evaluate the role and opposition of the members of the Eritrean Assembly during the period of the Federation.
5. Discuss the advantages and disadvantages of the secretive recruitment of ELM, and compare that with the development of Eritrean national struggle for independence.
6. Could Eritrean independence have been achieved only by the political struggle of the 1940s and 1950s? Discuss this.

Lesson 25:

Grounds/*Reasons* for the Start of the Armed Struggle

Lesson Goals:

By the end of this lesson, students will gain a basic understanding of the following:

1. Repressive measures of the Ethiopian government against peaceful resistance of the Eritrean people and activities of the E.L.M. (Eritrean Liberation Movement, *hereafter ELM*)

2. The exhaustion *of* peaceful political struggle

3. Cultural and artistic expression of the population's opposition to the violation of the Federal Agreement and the ineffectiveness of the Eritrean Assembly (lamentation)

4. Exile of Eritrean leaders and students

5. The birth of the E.L.F. (Eritrean Liberation Front, *hereafter ELF*)

The exhaustion *of* peaceful political struggle

- In the previous book we saw how Eritreans in the second half the 1950s were showing massive resistance against an *ever-growing* Ethiopian interference and hegemonic tendencies

- Ethiopia on its part was using force to suppress this growing resistance. It is thus important to repeat what we have read before about the violation of the federation and the resistance against this violation.

- In 1957-58 there were massive workers and students demonstrations involving thousands of people. *Ethiopian* response to these peaceful demonstrations was with massive repressive force. As a result, hundreds were killed or wounded and thousands of demonstrators were arrested.

- Despite all these, the Eritrean public didn't abandon the struggle it was waging to gain its national right. In October of 1957, qenezmach Omar Qadi presented a memorandum to the UN General Assembly in New York opposing Ethiopian steps. The UN didn't reply, but Omar Qadi was sentenced to ten year imprisonment when he came back from New York.

- Similarly several political leaders who opposed Ethiopia were becoming a target to harassment and imprisonment and many of them were forced into exile. Under such a situation, Sheikh Ibrahim Sultan and Idris Mohammed Adem were forced into exile in Egypt.

- *The ELM,which* was founded in November of 1958, spread its organizational activities across Eritrea and laid a national ground for resistance by recruiting workers and students. In 1962 it managed to organize a massive demonstration in Asmara opposing the violation of the federation. The police tried to break it up by force and several key *ELM* leaders were arrested.

- In general as Eritrean resistance grew Ethiopian repression and intimidation also grew proportionally and let alone to hold demonstrations opposing Ethiopia, even holding a meeting of four or five people became impossible. All avenues to a peaceful resistance were closed. And even the *ELM* that was in a better organizational position to exploit the ripe conditions for the start of an armed struggled failed to do so for lack of a clear political program.

Resistance and *Artistic shows*

- The Eritrean public was not *only* expressing its opposition to the violation of the federation and the actions leading to it through its

105

public demonstrations that were being repressed by the use of force, but *also* through the lyrics of the songs staged *in cinemas* by its artists as well.

- One of the earliest songs had lyrics lamenting Eritrean political leaders exile with the following words:

  > Asmeret my dear, ripe like a grape
  >
  > I am gloomy because of your fate
  >
  > I am gone pursuing the clouds
  >
  > Forget the love we had going
  >
  > The sun is rising out of the clouds
  >
  > Gone are the days of our togetherness
  >
  > Get me a memorabilia to wear on my wrist
  >
  > I am gone no one will detain me
  >
  > I am worried *and* sick about our relationship
  >
  > Lest it ages like cloth wilts like a leaf

- In the above song the word "asmeret" is referring to Asmara. The two words share the same root which means "unity".

- Another song that expressed the ineptitude of the Eritrean Assembly went like this

  > Assembly members adjudicate in truth
  >
  > So that you can safely come down from high places

- the following was sang to express the coming of Ethiopian rule in violation of the federation

  > Pass me my torch
  >
  > Don't discriminate

Don't deceive me

- And in the following Tigre song the forced federation of Eritrea with Ethiopia is represented with the forced marriage of a young girl to an old man.

sebr wdey etishfegi patience, don't rush	Have
beAl sebr Ewut tu patient wins	Who she is
yetimet ma mn enti you're an orphan	Even though
yetim Haqu baditu given to the orphan	No justice is
we n'shuma mn enti you are petite	Even though
n'ush Haqu slub tu petite is stolen	Right of the
sebr wdey etishfegi patience, don't rush	Have
shebabtki duly tu are ready.	Your youth
Hanuneche Ajuz tu is very old	My husband
lemraQo kalesa finished his fluids	He has
emenini abier tu is ancient	Believe me he
enjabuma 'tkefkafa all fallen	His teeth have
Hanunche gndab tu Achmetu tASefa is old, his bones are frail	My husband
it'men we itemeni Do not believe it	

wela eb 'br aKrafa   He is truely

wasted by old age

- These songs that directly and indirectly were expressing opposition to Ethiopia had a long lasting impact in raising the political consciousness and boosting the spirit of the struggle.

The Founding/*Establishment* of the Eritrean Liberation Front

- Those students who were doing their studies in Arabic were continuing their education in Arab countries, particularly Egypt. This was possible because *the Egypt was led by Gamal Abdel Nasser under an "Arab Socialist Republic" system, which* had opened a big opportunity where students coming from Africa and the Middle East can study under a scholarship.

- Particularly, after Amharic became the medium of instruction, the number of *Eritrean* students going to exile grew by many folds. As a result of this, in 1960, there about 400 Eritrean students pursuing their university and high school education in Cairo. Earlier in 1953, the Eritrean Students Club had been established. In 1959 it was renamed Eritrean Student Union.

- As it was explained earlier, in the 1940s and 1950s, Eritrean political leaders such as: Woldeab Woldemariam, Sheikh Ibrahim Sultan and Idris Mohammed Adem were exiled to Egypt and were, each on his own, continuing with their political agitations.

- As a result of these, in the beginning of the 1960s, amongst those Eritreans in Egypt, particularly in Cairo where an intense revolutionary *movement* of Africa and the Middle East was going on, political activities was on the rise.

- At this time, Idris Mohammed Adem, because he saw the Eritrean Liberation Movement as a secular and socialist movement, he was not willing to work with it. In addition because he had political differences with Woldeab Woldemariam and Sheikh Ibrahim Sultan dating back to the 1940s, he was not ready to work with them. Thus, he started raising funds from the Eritrean community to enable him start his own political organization.

- People like Seid Hussein and Idris Gelawdiyos, key leaders of the Eritrean Student Union, sided with Idris Mohammed Adem.

- In this manner, *in* July 1960, Idris Mohammed Adem together with some members of the Eritrean Student Union like: Seid Hussein Adem, Idris Osman Gelawdiyos, Mohammed Saleh Humed, Mohammed Akete, Taha Mohammed Nur and others, founded/*established* the Eritrean Liberation Front (*ELF*). *They* proclaimed that the goal of the *ELF was* to liberate Eritrea through an armed struggle.

- All those who participated in the founding meeting became members of the executive committee of the organization. After Osman Saleh Sabe, who was then in Jeddah, joined the organization in 1961 at the urging of Idris Mohammed Adem, a trio: Idris Mohammed Adem (as Chairman), Idris Osman Gelawdiyos (as Secretary) and Osman Saleh Sabe (as Secretary of Foreign Relations) started to control the Organization.

Questions

1. List major examples of peaceful resistance of the Eritrean public against the abrogation of the Federation.

2. What was the reason many Eritrean students were going into exile in Egypt?

3. Why did Idris Mohammed Adem and his supporters decide to establish a new organization?

Lesson 26:

The Start of the Armed Struggle

Lesson Goals:

By the end of this lesson, students will gain a basic understanding of the following:

- Preparations for the commencement of the armed struggle and Awate's initiative in the history of the history of the Eritrean Armed Struggle;

- The organizational and command structure of the *ELF* from 1961 to 1965

- Military developments inside Eritrea and the liquidation of the *ELM* (161-1965)

- Emperor Haile Selassie's initial military and diplomatic handling and *the* outlook of the Eritrean Armed Struggle (banditry, Arabism, *and* secessionist)

Hamid Idris Awate's Initiative in the History of the Armed Struggle:

- After the ELF was founded in Cairo in the manner we saw above, it started looking for people inside Eritrea and the Sudan to help it spearhead the Armed Struggle.

- At the time ~~since~~ Hamid Idris Awate was ready to spearhead the Armed Struggle, *he started it with* seven *of his* comrades *who had six* old rifles, and they went into *the "bush" [mountainous areas]* to commence the Armed Struggle. As a result of the confrontation

110

he had with the Ethiopians at Mt. Adal on September 1, 1961, this date was taken as the official **starting date of the** Eritrean Armed Struggle for Independence.

- Hamid Idris Awate was born in 1911. He had served with the Italian colonial army from the 1930s until its defeat in 1941. He had received military training in Rome and had a command of the Italian language. During the British Military Administration in Eritrea, he was **in the "Bush" [mountainous areas]** defending the people of Barka from Beja and Ethiopian-trained bandit raids. As a result, he had gained more military experience. After the British Amnesty declaration of 1951, he returned to a civilian life and was living as a farmer until 1961.

Hamid Idris Awate

Mt. Adal (Gash Barka) where the first shot for independence was fired.

- He died of an illness in June of 1962; however, because of the fame he had gained, **which** was a source of inspiration to *tegadelti* and the public, it was decided to keep the news of his martyrdom in secrecy. Even those who succeeded him were presented **as** *his*lieutenants or second-in-command. For a long time, the myth about Awate's ability continued to serve as an inspiration to *tegadelti* and *the* population alike. There were plenty of stories that went like: "how he had *a* charm or talisman that protected him from bullets, magical power that enabled him to be invisible in a plain sight, he could *also* jump like an antelope, is a marksman who never misses his target, etc. …"

ELF: Organizational Structure and Leadership (1961-1965)

- In the history of the first decade of the Armed Struggle, the ELF continued as the sole organization in the Eritrean field. However. *However, at the time,* the organization had neither a coherent political program nor a clear organizational structure or leadership.

- In the pinnacle of power of the organization was the *self-appointed* Supreme Council. This group was based in Cairo, Egypt. Its key members were: Idris Mohammed Adem, Idris Osman Gelawdiyos and Osman Saleh Sabe.

Idris Osman GelawdiyosIdris Mohammed AdemOsman Saleh Sabe

- After the martyrdom of Hamid Idris Awate's due to illness, command of the Eritrean Liberation Army *(hereafter ELA)* in the field passed, respectively to Mohammed Idris Haj, to Mohammed Omar Abdalla (abu Tiyara), and Abubaker Mohammed Idris.

However, after the martyrdom of Abubaker, the command of ELA was centralized under the leadership of Tahir Salim who *was*based in Kassala, Sudan, and Mahmud Dinai in the Eritrean field. This continued until the formation of Zonal/*regional* commands.

- In the 1960s, the ELF didn't have a clear and detailed revolutionary program and strategy that went beyond the general goal of liberating Eritrea through an armed struggle. On one hand, since the political outlook of the ELF leadership was based on the narrow regional and religious divisions of the 1940s, and on the other hand because they didn't have a desire to bring about a revolutionary change to the Eritrean society, together with their narrow sectarian outlook, they were not able to produce a revolutionary national leadership that could guide the revolution. This was vividly visible in the divisive and regionalist policies they were following.

- The need for a political program and strategy that ensures unity and independence is a fundamental requirement of any struggle. We are going to see the price the Eritrean Revolution was forced to expend due to the lack of such a political program and strategy in the early stages of the Armed Struggle.

- Between 1961 and 1965 the ELF had managed to spread its organization all over Eritrea particularly inside the big cities. These nationalists that were organized in secret, taking a lesson from the organizational structure of the Eritrean Liberation Movement (ELM) or "Haraka" [in Arabic] were performing their activities by organizing themselves in cells. The main function of these cells *was* intelligence gathering, recruiting new members, and raising funds. There were several similar ELF cells in the neighboring countries such as: Saudi Arabia and the Sudan. Their main function was mobilizing support for the Eritrean Revolution.

113

Military Developments in the Eritrean Field

- It didn't take long for the news of the commencement of the Armed Struggle to spread all over Eritrea. The population started expressing its support in many ways and many nationalists started making contacts with the Revolution.

- *In* March of 1962, nine Eritrean members of the Sudanese Army joined the Armed Struggle. These were followed by several Eritrean soldiers and civilian workers ~~*that*~~ *who* were in the Sudan. This was also bolstered by the defection of *some* members of the Eritrean Field Police force *in Eritrea and joined* the ranks of the Armed Struggle. This brought a visible change to the ranks of the first Awate unit.

From the First Unit of Tegadelti (Freedom Fighters)

- Due to the limit that existed in terms of the number of *tegadelti* and arms, it was impossible to confront the enemy *face-to-face* in the beginning. As a result, the strategy was based on *hit-and-*

114

*run*guerrilla warfare. They used to take their mission in smaller units and most of the early operations were limited to targeting remote enemy police stations and stores in the Gash-Barka area. Based on this tactic, the Revolution, despite the limitations and shortages it faced, it had managed to score important victories. *As a result,* it was able to capture a good number of enemy rifles. The time-honored Eritrean tradition and maxim of the Armed Struggle that said: "fighting the enemy with its own rifles and bullets" has its roots in these early encounters and raids.

- We can list the following famous operations from the early 1960s

  a) **The Akurdet Operation (July 12, 1962)**: This was a grenade attack that took place in a meeting, in a broad day light, in the middle of Akurdet, *which* was being *led* by the Ethiopian General Abiye Abebe, and the Chief Executive of the Eritrean Administration, Asfeha Woldemichael, and attended by several Ethiopian government officials. This attack killed 4 enemy officials, including the Secretary of Law and Justice of the Eritrean Administration, Mohammed Omar Haseno. There were also 31 people *who* were wounded by the attack.

  b) **The Battle of Anseba (January 1963)**: This was an attack that captured 11 rifles.

  c) **The Battle of Jengerien (March 8, 1963):** This attack captured 23 rifles and 2 Bren machine guns.

  d) **The Hykota Operation (June 28, 1963):** This was a remarkable operation that took place at noon, when *tegadelti* coming in civilian *clothes* and *in a bus*, attacked a police station. They managed to capture over 20 guns.

e) **The Battle of Togorba (March 1964):** This was the first battle against the Ethiopian Army. As a result, it had a political significance. At the time, it was the biggest battle that lasted for hours. In this battle, 17 *tegadelti* were martyred and the enemy lost even more.

- At the end of 1964, ELA units were strengthened by **numerous students and workers who** joined their ranks. In 1963, there were only 4 ELA units; in 1964, this increased to 7. In the same year, the first round of Syrian-trained *tegadelti,* armed with modern weapons, came back to the field. In 1965, the number of *tegadelti* in the field was in the hundreds.

Haile Selassie's Initial Diplomatic and Military Policies

- Contrary to the popularity, influence and strength of the Eritrean Revolution that was growing day by day, Haile Selassie's initial reaction was to deny the very existence of such an Eritrean Revolution. All *of* its earlier efforts were aimed at hiding the reality of an Armed Struggle inside Eritrea from the world. Ethiopian government diplomatic organs attempted to deprive the Eritrean Revolution its due credit by presenting it as if it was an act of banditry.

- From *a* military angle, it sought to eliminate the Eritrean Revolution by deploying first units of the Eritrean Field Force, and then by mobilizing the Ethiopian regular army. The support it was getting from the Israelis and the Americans helped it intensify its military campaigns.

- After it was getting crystal clear the Armed Struggle of the Eritrean people was a question of a national liberation from a colonial rule, the Ethiopian government attempted to present it as if it was a move sponsored Arab enemies of Ethiopia and has no national support. It tried an old political tradition, one that attempts to sow religious discord in the population, by claiming that Ethiopia was a "Christian island amid an Islamic sea" and the Eritrean rebellion was not one of national liberation, but a religious (Islamic) rebellion.

- In the African arena, the issue was presented as a secessionist movement to the Organization of African Unity *[hereafter OAU]*, whose principle was against secession). It argued that it was an internal Ethiopian matter and against the OAU principle of "non-interference in the internal affairs of other states". We will present all these ever changing military and diplomatic policies of Ethiopia in subsequent lessons.

The Eritrean Liberation Movement (Haraka) in the Field

- Ever since the founding of the ELF in 1960, the political differences between the leaders of the *ELM* and the *ELF* began widening. When the ELF began the Armed Struggle, and as they saw the political influence of the ELM waning, ELM leaders began to repeatedly call for unity. However, all these calls were given a deaf ear by the ELF leadership.

- As a result of this, the ELM leaders decided to start their own armed struggle and dispatched a 50-*tegadelti* force into Sahel. However, since the ELF leadership had taken a stand that said "the Eritrean arena cannot carry more than one organization", they attacked the ELM force at a place called Illa Saeda, near Karora. In this encounter (civil war), 4 ELM tegadelti were killed and the rest of them were forced to lay down their arms. With this, the military presence of the ELM inside Eritrea ended in 1965.

- After this incident, key ELM members such as Saleh Iyay chose to join the ELF, and the ELM *remnants led* by Mohammed Seid

117

Nawd joined the *"Amna Ama"*, which was *led* by Osman Saleh Sabe in the 1970s.

Questions

1. Explain the organizational and leadership weakness of the ELF.

2. Explain the maxim "fighting the enemy with its own rifles and bullets" by relating it to the first ELA operations.

3. Give an account of what the initial Ethiopian military and diplomatic reaction was to the beginning of the Eritrean Armed Struggle.

Lesson 27:

The Era of Zonal/*Regional* Commands (1965-1968)

Lesson Goals:

By the end of this lesson, students will gain a basic understanding of the following:

- The Kassala congress of the ELF and the ensuing change that came to the organizational and military structures of the ELF.

- The declared reason for establishing the *zonal/regional* commands

- The consequence of the creation of the *zonal/regional* commands

The Establishment of the Zonal Commands

- In the history of the Eritrean Armed Struggle what is referred to as the "era of zonal/*regional* commands" is the time when the ELA was divided into 5 independent zonal/regional commands that had a clearly designated operational zone.

- On July 20, 1965, the Supreme Council together with representatives that came from inside the field and other countries held a congress in Kassala, Eastern Sudan.

- The official reason the Supreme Council gave for the need to restructure the military structure was the fact that the majority of the ELA units were confined to the western lowlands and this:

a) Was creating a minimal threat to the continued colonial existence of the Ethiopian regime in Eritrea.

b) *Was a* burden of supplying the units with food, ***which*** was beyond the capacity of the local population.

- The establishment of the zonal/regional commands was taken from the experience of the Algerian Revolution. As a result, the Kassala Congress divided the ELA into 4 zonal commands, and as the number of Tigrigna speaking tegadelti grew, a 5th zonal command was added in 1966 to accommodate them.

- Every commander of a zone was chosen to be from the zone he represented. The 1st zone in Barka was led by Mahmud Dinai, the 2nd zone around Sahel and Senhit was under Omar Izaz, the 3rd zone covering Seraye and Hamasien was under the leadership of Abdelkerim Ahmed, the 4th zone in Semhar and Denkel was led by Mohammed Ali Omaro, and the 5th and final zonal command was under Wolday Kahsai.

- In addition, the Congress created a Kassala-based Revolutionary Command that linked the Supreme Council with the zonal commands in the field. Saad Adem was appointed to head the Revolutionary Command. Furthermore, two units, one for training and another for reserve force, were established and Omar Damir and Mohammed Omar Abdalla (abu Tiyara), in that order, were appointed to oversee their activities.

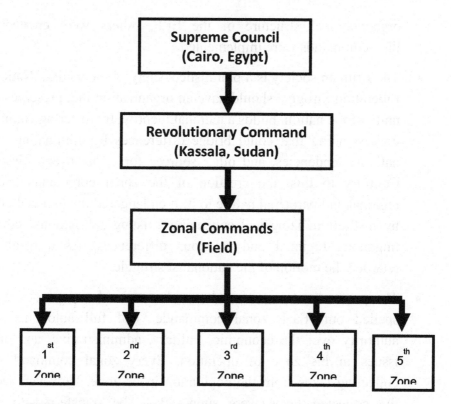

ELF's Organizational Structure During the Era of Zonal Commands

The Consequence of the Zonal Command Era

- The establishment of the zonal commands made ELA units to operate over a wider area and in densely populated areas. This forced the enemy to over stretch itself and become less effective, and as a result was exposed to more attacks. The news of the different encounters with the Ethiopian colonial army played a positive role in building the reputation of the revolution as well as in increasing the number of those who were joining the ranks of the ELA.

- Nevertheless, the establishment of the zonal commands had created a dangerous situation that had risked the possible endof the Armed Struggle. Part of it was due to the inherent weakness of the

121

organizational structure of the ELF, others were created as thesecommands were implemented.

- The Eritrean society is a pluralistic society. As a result, a National Liberation Struggle should have an organization that preserves the unity of the nation, builds a national identity, by fostering common understanding that could bridge differences by eliminating sub-national tendencies, and other sources for division and discord. Contrary to this, the creation of the zonal commands had a regional and parochial nature to it. It endangered the national unity by institutionalizing and enhancing existing sub-national ethnic, linguistic, regional and religious differences. As a result, it retarded the motion of the nationalist struggle.

- The power limitation of each zonal commander was not clearly spelled out. Each zonal commander had full autonomy and authority over the economic, military, administrative, and other issues in his zone of operation. Every zonal command was collecting taxes from the population in its zone. However, while the collected taxes were supposed to be transferred to and administered by the Revolutionary Command in Kassala, zonal commanders were unwilling to do so, preferring to administer their own revenues by themselves. Realizing that, a greater economic power leads to a greater power to dominate, their focus became tax collection, neglecting other revolutionary tasks.

- Zonal commanders used to take unjust actions that abused and ill-treated the population. To mention a couple heinous crimes: in 1967 Ethiopia had burned the village of Adi Ibrahim. In July 1967, by claiming the Kunama had collaborated with the Ethiopians, the first zonal command of the ELF retaliated by burning Kunama villages and murdering about 30 Kunamas. This forced members of the Kunama community to seek refuge with the enemy, and to carry arms on behalf of the enemy. On October of the same year, this very same zonal command killed 43 farmers from the Anseba region *who* had come to farm in the Gash valley. These and similar incidents had enabled the Ethiopian government get some support for its cause.

- In the Toraa-Tsinadegle dispute that originally started as a disagreement over land use, leaders of the 3rd zone escalated the conflict by taking side with the Toraa. Ethiopia on its part tried to exploit this opportunity and used it to arm the Tsinadegle.

- According to the declaration of the Kassala Congress, each zonal command was not supposed to have more than 30% of its tegadelti *from* a single ethnic group. The zonal commanders on the other hand started recruiting and training tegadelti on their own bypassing the central department, *which was* tasked with training. As a result, the units in the zonal commands were being dominated by members from a single ethnic group.

- In practice, the zonal commanders turned into War Lords and units in the zonal commands, instead of becoming national units, they became bastion of ethnic and regional divisions. This in turn brought a clash among the zones, *which was* a result of the desire to increase their influence and widen their territory.

- There was no institutional channel of communication between the Supreme Council, the Revolutionary Command, and the Zonal Commands. On top of this, there was a major rivalry for power among members of the Supreme Council fostering polarization. The three top leaders of the Supreme Council used the 1st, 2nd, and 4th zones as their power base, and started to have a direct and personal relationship, based on regional affinities.

- There was a patron and client relationship between members of the Supreme Council and affiliated zonal commands. The patron in the Supreme Council provided arms and logistics to the zone affiliated with him, and the zonal command as a client was serving the *interests* of its patron in the field. This kind of relationship further divided and paralyzed the ELF.

- Idris Mohammed Adem, and Idris Osman Gelawdiyos, in that order, were patrons for the 1st and 2nd zonal commands. Since these two commands were based in the part of Eritrea where the Armed Struggle started, relative to the other zones they were in a better position. The 4th zone for its part was the client of Osman Saleh Sabe. The 3rd and 5th commands on the other hand were at a disadvantage because they had no patron in the Supreme Council.

- Under this circumstance, the Revolutionary Command that was meant to be a bridge between the Supreme Council and the zonal commands was totally sidelined and became part of the parochial divisions.

- In general, the absence of a political program on one hand and a divisive regionalist relationship from the other side were proof to the organizational failure of the ELF. As a result, the zonal commands were immersed into competition instead of coordination and unity. This was exhibited vividly during the 1967 scorched-earth campaign of the Ethiopian government.

Questions

1. Give the reasons given by the ELF leadership why they created the zonal commands

2. Explain organizational structure of the ELF that existed during the era of zonal commands.

3. List the major problems that surfaced with the establishment of the zonal commands.

Lesson 28:

Ethiopia's Political and Military Campaigns

Lesson Goals:

By the end of this lesson, students will gain a basic understanding of the following:

- People's peaceful resistance and Ethiopia's violent response.

- Ethiopia's scorched-earth military campaign and the suffering it brought on the Eritrean population.

Public Resistance and Ethiopian Conspiracy

- At a time when the situation in the field was taking a wrong direction, the ELF cells in the cities were busy recruiting members and student demonstrations were on the rise.

- In March of 1965, thousands of students *took off to* the streets of Asmara to condemn Ethiopian occupation of Eritrea. This was a big threat to Ethiopian rule and Haile Selassie's response was to arrest hundreds of peaceful students who were involved in the demonstrations. *The students'* demands were:

  a) The UN should condemn Ethiopian occupation

  b) A referendum deciding Eritrea's future should be held

125

c) American and Israeli soldiers should leave Eritrea and America should vacate the Kagnew Communication base.

d) All political prisoners need to be released

e) The closure of factories should come to an end.

- After this incident, a direct relationship between the students in Asmara and the ELF was established. Many of those nationalist students who established ELF cells in 1966 at the Haile Sellasie I University (now Addis Ababa University) were later to play key leadership *roles* in the Eritrean Revolution.

- In 1965/1966, Eritrean cities saw massive unprecedented student mobilization against Ethiopian occupation. As Ethiopia started to crack down on these students, many of them joined the ranks of the ELF.

- This kind of popular movement was a big slap to the Haile Sellasie regime of Ethiopia that it was trying to present the Eritrean Revolution, *at times as banditry, and other times as an Arab instigated rebellion.* Realizing that the Eritrean police force cannot destroy the Eritrean Revolution, it was forced to increase its military power and in some areas it declared a state of emergency law.

- In order to pit Eritreans against each other, Ethiopia started recruiting Christian youth from the highlands and trained them as a counter-insurgency police commando force. This commando force was trained by the *Israelis*. Starting from the first class of September 1964, *all of* the major Ethiopian military campaigns against the Eritrean Revolution until 1975, this force was the primary force. The Ethiopian standing policy was to divide the

126

Eritrean population along religious and regional lines, rendering it impossible to fight for its right in unison. The conscious response of the Eritrean public to this dangerous divisive policy can better be summarized by the lyrics of the following song that called for unity:

> *Christians* or Moslems of the highlands or lowlands
> Don't give weight to enemy's advice
> Don't give it weight, lest you become a bargaining chip.

Ethiopia's Scorched-earth Campaign

- In 1967 Ethiopia started a scorched-earth campaign to destroy the Eritrean Revolution. This campaign started *in March 1967*. Before this time, the 2nd Division of the Ethiopian *Armywas based* in Eritrea and had a size of one brigade. *However, after this broad campaign,* the remaining two brigades were mobilized to Eritrea. The police commando force was also involved in the campaign.

- During the 1967 Ethiopian scorched-earth campaign, hundreds of Eritrean villages were torched and thousands of innocent civilians were murdered. In the upper Barka region alone, 62 villages were burned and around 300 people were killed. Several villages were burned in the Hazemo plain and over 253 civilians were killed. On top of these, 30 villages were burned in Sahel and Senhit areas, and many people were *also* killed. In a similar destructive campaign, the Ethiopian army murdered over 115 people in Semhar. As a result of all these, around 30 thousand citizens were forced into the Sudan as refugees. This was the first waves of refugees. By the time of independence, the number of refugees in the Sudan and other countries had swelled to *about 500,000* or half a million.

Ethiopia's Way of Intimidating Civilians
Hanging bodies of Tegadelti Killed in Battle (Keren mid 1960s)

Questions

1. What were the demands of the student demonstrations of 1965?
2. In the mid-1960s, what tactics did the Haile Sellasie regime use to "divide and rule" Eritrea? What was its purpose?
3. What does scorched-earth policy mean?

Lesson 29:

The Rectification Movement (*Islah, in Arabic*)

Lesson Goals:

By the end of this lesson, students will gain a basic understanding of the following:

- Immediate and fundamental reasons for rectification.

- The process of rectification (the initiators and its origins: the Aredaib, Anseba and Adobha conferences).

- The outcome of the Rectification Movement: its victories and failures.

The Origins of the Rectification Movement (Islah)

- The Ethiopian campaign and the destruction and atrocities it brought on the civilian population had a negative military impact on the ELF. It highlighted the weaknesses of the zonal command structuring of the ELA. The absence of coordination between the zonal commands had rendered the ELF weak and unable to protect the civilians or defend itself.

- For example, since the 3rd and 5th zonal commands were unable to stop the enemy that moved in the areas, they were forced to retreat to the area of other zones. The remaining three zonal commands as well didn't have a military plan or strategy to fend off the enemy.

- Under such chaotic circumstances, nationalist democratic *tegadelti* [freedom fighters, in Tigrigna] started a campaign for change. Most of those tegadletis campaigning for change were once students or workers *in the cities*. While their primary goal was to get rid off the

129

zonal command structure, they were also opposed *to* the unrepresentative and absentee Supreme Council.

- As a result, *within* the ELF a movement called the *Rectification Movement* or *Islah* started. After this movement was initiated by some reform-minded revolutionary tegadelti, it was well received among the rank and file members of the ELF.

- Through the initiation of the leaders of the 3rd and 5th zones that were forced out of their zones, a meeting of all leaders of the zones was held on 16 June 1968 at Aradaib. At Aradiab, the following proposal was *submitted* by those tegadelti in the Islah or Rectification Movement.

  - *Create* a unified army by eliminating the zonal commands

  - *Have* the leadership to be inside the field

  - The population's rights must be respected; it should be left to administer itself by electing its own leaders and participate in the revolution.

- In order to reach a decision by debating the proposal, it was decided to hold a conference where all the zonal commands will be present. The leaders of the 1st and 2nd zonal commands who were opposed to the process failed to show up for the three consecutive meetings scheduled for the 21st of July, 1st September and the 10th of September of 1968.

The Anseba Conference

- After the three appointed meetings failed *to* materialize, the leaders and cadres of the 3rd, 4th and 5th zones met on September 19, 1968, at a place called Orotta in what is now referred as the Anseba Conference. At this meeting, they formed what is called the Tripartite Union. This union was joined by the training and reserve units. This Tripartite Union elected a 12-member[1] provisional revolutionary council.

- Members of the Supreme Council, objecting the formation of the Tripartite Union, refused to recognize *its* new leadership.

- Ethiopia on its part decided to kill this force from its inception and launched an offensive. However, the Tripartite Union force was strong enough to repulse the enemy's attack. On top of this, it managed in a short period *of time* to launch several operations against the enemy, and this underscored the advantage of having a united force.

- Since the 1st and 2nd zones expressed their acceptance of unity a new meeting was called.

The Adobha Conference

- This conference was designed to unite the 1st and 2nd zones with the Tripartite Union ensuring a total merger of the whole ELA. Representatives that were elected from the Tripartite Union, along with those that were delegated from the 1st and 2nd zones participated in the meeting and agreed to unite the five zonal commands. Due to the pressure of the democratic elements at the Adobha Conference, the following democratic resolutions were adopted:

    o To hold a National Congress within one year

    o To form a preparatory committee for the proposed National Congress

---

[1] Its members were: 1. Mohammed Ahmed Abdu, 2. Mohammed Ali Omaru, 3. Isaias Afwerki, 4. Romadan Mohammed Nur, 5. Omar Damir, 6. Abraham Tewelde, 7. Abdela Safi, 8. Abdela Yosuf, 9. Ahmed Ibrahim, 10. Hamid Saleh, 11. Abdella Idris, 12. Mohammed Omar Abdella.

- To appoint a committee that investigates the atrocities that were committed upon tegadelti as well as the population.

- Members of the Supreme Council to stay in power until the National Congress. However, their power will be limited and the Revolutionary Command will be disbanded.

- Zonal commanders and their deputies shouldn't be given any role.

- A 38-member General Command was established. *Eighteen [18]* of them were elected members from the Tripartite Union, and 20 were selected from the delegates of the 1st and 2nd*divisions*. Since the membership of the General Command was the result of a lot of compromises, it didn't reflect the democratic spirit of the rectification movement. This was manifested shortly by the actions the General Command took and its aftermath.

- After the Adobha Conference, the General Command under the chairmanship of Mohammed Ahmed Abdu took control of the ELA. However, the General Command was not ready to work for the reform of the Revolution. Since it was dominated by reactionaries and divisive elements, it didn't bother to implement the democratic resolutions of the Adobha Conference.

- Opposition to the General Command started coming from different quarters, including its own members. Rejecting the General Command, in November 1969, Osman Saleh Sabe and his followers met in Aman, Jordan, and formed the General Secretariat. The General Command's response to this was to get rid *off* the Supreme Council. Five members of the General Command who opposed this move were arrested.

- In less than a year, in violation of the decision of the Adobha Conference, the General Command executed several tegadelti,

132

including Kidane Kiflu and Wolday Ghidey; it dissolved the preparatory and investigative committees that were established at the Conference. Furthermore, it reinstated the leadership of the zonal commands to power.

- The General Command disarmed and dismissed hundreds of tegadelti that opposed it and it killed several. Under *an* atmosphere of intimidation and harassment, several tegadelti who were members of the rectification movement reached the conclusion that "no change could come by working within the ELF", and they started abandoning the Front.

- While the field, *under such* chaotic circumstances, there were *some* tegadelti who performed a heroic *act* and brought international attention and recognition of the Eritrean Revolution. Some of these activities were attacks on Ethiopian airlines in Karachi (Pakistan), Frankfurt (Germany) and Rome (Italy), and another Ethiopian airlines plane was hijacked while in flight.

- Similarly, tegadelti attacked *the trains* along the Asmara-Akurdet line. Along the Asmara-Keren road, at a place called Balwa, the Commander of Ethiopia's 2nd Division, General Teshome Ergetu, was killed in a tegadelti ambush. *Unnerved* by this action, the Haile Sellasie Regime decided to get out its revenge on peaceful civilians. On 31 December 1970, they burned the village of Ona (2 km outside Keren) and committed an unprecedented mass murder, killing 750 people among *whom* were children and the elderly, and 100 others were wounded. They also executed another 57 youth from the surrounding, who opposed the *massacre*. This raised the total number of victims to 807. Before that, on 30 November 1970, a total of 131 innocent civilians, 50 among them underage children, Moslems and Christians who had taken refuge inside a mosque, were murdered at the village of Besgedira (not far from Keren). These *massacres* initiated another wave of Eritrean refugees into the Sudan. Earlier in 1969, there was another wave of refugees who escaped into the Sudan. The first wave, however, had fled to the Sudan to escape an indiscriminate bombing of civilians by the Ethiopian army. They were from the eastern lowlands and eastern Akele-guzai.

A Train Destroyed by Tegadelti

- In addition, the students' movement inside Eritrea and Ethiopia was in the increase. For instance, in 1969, Eritrean students at *The* Bahri-Dar (Northwest Ethiopia) *Polytechnic* Institute started protesting. All secondary school students in Eritrea started protesting in support of these Eritrean students, who were expelled from the Ethiopian Polytechnic. This demonstration was bigger than the one in 1965. The 1972-73 year long boycott of all secondary school education also showed the strength and organization of the *students'* movement.

- Finally in 1970, the Haile Sellasie Regime declared a state of emergency, and the whole of Eritrea was put under a military administration. The curfew that started at this time continued up to the time of independence. The civilian administrator of Eritrea, Prince Asrat Kassa, was replaced by General Debebe Hailemariam, who was commander of the *Imperial Bodyguard.*

Questions

1. What was the direct reason that strengthened the Rectification Movement?
2. What was the outcome of the Anseba Conference?
3. Explain briefly about the Adobha Conference and its *outcomes.*
4. Mention some of the major operations that were carried by tgadelti between 1969 and 1970. What was the major significance of these operations?

Lesson 30:
Question and Discussion Period

Discussion in groups
- Every classroom forms groups, with each group electing a chairperson and secretary and discussing on assigned topics. A summary of the discussion is then presented to the class.
- Assuming a period is 60 minutes long, 25 minutes are allocated for the discussion part and the remaining 35 minutes for the group presentations.uestions for discussion (needs to be answered in groups):

Points for discussion (to be answered in groups):

- The songs that were directly and indirectly reflecting the population's defiance and resistance had a long lasting influence on raising national awareness and in cultivating the spirit of the struggle. How *was this possible*? Discuss it.
- The ELF leadership had *a position that stated*: "the Eritrean Revolution cannot afford to have more than one organization". What is your *opinion about this position?*
- We say the formation of the zonal commands didn't take the objective reality in Eritrea. *Why was this so?* Discuss it.
- One consequence of the war and enemy rule is the increase in the number of refugees that *fled* their country. Discuss the consequence and impact it had on the social, and economic fabric of *the* society
- Eritrean student organizations had played a crucial role in the success of the national struggle. Explain this by giving examples.

Lesson 31:

The Eritrean People's Liberation Forces [hereafter EPLF]: Birth and Growth

Lesson Goals:

By the end of this lesson, students will gain a basic understanding of the following:

- The process of *the split* of different groups from the ELF.

- The First National Congress of the ELF and its reaction to the split.

- The start of the civil war and the regrouping of the different opposition groups

- The *EPLF*: birth and growth.

- The end of the civil war

The Eritrean People's Liberation Forces (EPL Forces), *which* later was renamed the Eritrean People's Liberation Front (EPL Front), was the merger of three groups that split from the ELF The processes and times these three groups split from the ELF between 1970 and 1971 were different. In this lesson, we will see the process of the split and merger of *the* three groups

E.P.L. Forces: First Group

- All *of* the tegadelti who opposed the General Command were disarmed and dismissed, and *others* who escaped started regrouping in the Sudan, and looking for means to continue their

137

national struggle. These tegadelti, helped by Osman Saleh Sabe's General Secretariat, first flew from the Sudan to South Yemen, and then reentered into Eritrea through Dankalia. They crossed the Red Sea *by* boats.

- *This first group* that reentered into Eritrea held its first congress at Sodah Illa near Edi, and officially declared that it has split from the ELF, taking the name Eritrean People's Liberation Forces. *It elected* a 9-member[2] leadership team and *condemned* the General Command by *passing* the following resolutions

  o Oppose the anti-national stand of the General Command, and represent the interests of tegadelti and the population.

  o *Ensure* unity combating sectarian, religious, and regional tendencies

  o *Build* the political awareness of tegadelti and the population by providing regular education.

  o Not to recognize the General Secretariat or the Supreme Council, but accept Osman Saleh Sabe and Woldeab Woldemariam, not as representatives but *as* members.

- Shortly after the meeting at Sodah Illa, a split occurred within *the* first group. The disagreement came because of difference on where to have the base for the group. While the majority decided to remain in Southern Dankalia, a smaller group splintered and headed to Northern Sahel. However, the two subgroups merged again after they held a conference at Imba Hara (north of Keren in Habero) between 30 June and 9 July 1971. At this conference,

---

[2] These were: 1. Mohammed Ali Omaru, 2. Mesfin Hagos, 3. Maasho Embaye, 4. Mohammed Omar Abdalla (abu Tiyara), 5. Alamin Mohammed Said, 6. Mehari Debessay, 7. Omar Damir, 8. Mohammed Osman Ahmed and 9. Ali Mohammed Osman.

they elected a new leadership team chaired by Romadan Mohammed Nur and had Ahmed Hilal, Abubaker Mohammed Hassen, Saleh Tetew and Abubaker Mohammed Jimee as members.

- Osman Saleh Sabe, on one hand, because he was looking for a force inside Eritrea that he can call his own, and because the group didn't have access to food and supplies, an interest-based tactical alliance was established between Osman Saleh Sabe and this group.

EPL Forces: Second Group

- In March of 1970 another group (mostly highlanders) split from the ELF and regrouped around Alla. However, due to the pressures they were facing from the Ethiopian Government and the General Command in the plains of Alla, they decided to take refuge in the Semienawi Bahri forest.

- It first made contact with the first group in November of 1970 at a place called Simoti in northern Denkalia.

- The first contacts of this second group with the first group didn't lead to unity. *This was due* to the leftovers of mistrust and suspicion from the ELF. *Thus, the contact was* negatively affected and stalled the relationship between the two groups.

- After the relationship with the first group stalled, the second group held its own conference at a place called Tekli in Semienawi Bahri, *on 13-15* August, 1971. In this meeting, the group elected a 5-member leadership team chaired by Isaias Afwerki. At its Tekli meeting, the second group prepared a historical document titled *"we and our goals" (niHnan Elamanan)* that detailed the reasons it split from the ELF, and had the following principles:

- Oppose the undemocratic stand of the General Command

- Oppose all divisive tendencies that spring out of religious, ethnic, and regional pretexts, and never enter into alliances based on this.

- Struggle to bring about a society free of exploitation, and *fightagainst* the Ethiopian colonial rule by means of an armed struggle.

- Prepare a work plan that help coordinate with other national forces.

Third Group: Eritrean Liberation Forces (Ubel)

- This split of this group from the ELF was directly related *to* the power struggle that existed within the General Command. This group first met at the banks of the Ubel River (the name of the group is derived from this meeting venue) on 19 November 1970, and declared that it condemned the General Command, and will *no longer be bound* by its directives, and released the imprisoned members of the General Command.

- Its complete split from the ELF happened after *it failed to attend* at the Awete Military Conference (more on this later), *which was* called by the General Command. *On* 28 December 1971, the group met again in the Gash area and officially announced it has split from the E.L.F. and had taken the name Eritrean Liberation Forces, and elected and 11-member team led by Adem Saleh.

The Merger of the three Groups

- After the three groups established their presence in the Eritrean field in the manner we saw above, on January of 1972, *they* sent their representatives to Beirut, Lebanon, to seek help from Osman Saleh Sabe. The first group was represented by Romadan

140

Mohammed Nur and Ali Said Abdella, and the second group by Isaias Afwerki and Mesfin Hagos. Before they met with Osman Saleh Sabe, they had a bilateral meeting and agreed on the following points:

o The differences between them is secondary and can be resolved by having a joint meeting inside Eritrea

o The weapons and materials help they get will be split by a joint committee on need basis.

o A joint leadership committee will be created to draw a joint work plan, lead, and coordinate

o Darw a joint plan to bring about the merger of the two groups

o In communications with the General Secretariat to present themselves as a single body of Eritrean People's Liberation Forces.

• It was after this meeting *that* the two groups began to be called as first and second groups of the Eritrean People's Liberation Forces.

• In February of 1972, the two groups of the Eritrean People's Liberation Forces, the Eritrean Liberation Forces (Ubel) and Osman Saleh Sabe's General Secretariat held a meeting. It was agreed ~~that~~ to coordinate *their* work so that unity would be achieved, and a Congress can be held within a year. As for the General Secretariat*, it was decided to rename it* as the Foreign Mission of the Eritrean People's Liberation Forces, *and it would coordinate the needed work abroad, and transfer to the filed all aid (monetary and weapons) it receives from donors.*

From the First Eritrean Peoples' Liberation Forces Tegdaelti (Freedom Fighters)

The Civil War and the Establishment of the EPL Forces

- As we saw above, the General Command, under the pressure of the split of the three groups, called for a meeting called Awate Military Conference. While the call was rejected by the first and second groups of the EPLF, the Ubel group decided to participate. In this meeting, *which* lasted from 26 February and until March of 1971, it decided to hold a National Congress, and elected a preparatory Committee.

- On this basis, the ELF held its first National Congress between 14 October and 16 November 1971, at a place called Aar, along the north western part of the Eritrea-Sudan border.

- This first National Congress disbanded the General Command and replaced it by the Revolutionary Council and Executive Committee. The highest power of the organization rested with the Revolutionary Council. Idris Mohammed Adem and Hiruy Tedla Bairu were elected as Chairman and Deputy Chairman in that order.

142

- The ELF, at this congress, describing the Eritrean Revolution as a National Democratic Revolution, approved a political program that works for national unity, equality, and the enhancement of a revolutionary culture. Comparing it with the first ten years, this was a new chapter in the history of the ELF. However, the chairmanship of Idris Mohammed Adem was a manifestation of the continuation of the regionalist political alliance that was built in the 1960s.

- On the issue of the splinter groups, the Congress declaring that the "Eritrean field cannot accommodate more than one organization", ordered them to rejoin the ELF. *If the order was not obeyed*, on the other hand, *it gave* the power to the Revolutionary Council to take all *what it is* deemed necessary measures to ensure the safety of the Revolution.

- On this basis, on 24 February 1972, the Revolutionary Council decided to take a military action against the People's Liberation Forces. With this decision, a three-year old civil war started between the two organizations and brought *a heavy price upon the tegadelti.*

- The ELF's military action began by attacking the Eritrean Liberation Forces (Ubel) *on* 29 February 1972. With this attack, the military presence of the Ubel Forces inside Eritrea faced a temporary setback. Shortly after that, the ELF also attacked the first group of the People's Liberation Forces.

- After this attack, the second group that also knew that it will also be eventually attacked, (though the ELF had declared that it wouldn't attack the second group) joined the first group and retreated to Sahel. Later the two groups were joined by the remnants of the Ubel, group *that* reentered into Sahel by way of the Sudan.

143

- As the civil war going on, efforts were going on to bring about unity of the three groups of the EPL Forces. As a result, in October 1972, representatives of the three groups met at a place called Gihteb along the Eritrea-Sudan border, and elected an Administrative Committee that coordinates the political and military activities of the three groups. It was also agreed to convene a Congress that will also be joined by the Foreign Mission within six months, and bring about the unity of the three forces.

- At the beginning of 1973, the civil war restarted at a place called Ghereghir-Sudan, inside the Sudan. The war continued until the Sudanese army came in and stopped it. Through the mediation of the Sudanese Government, a meeting was held at Aghig and the ELF and the EPLF forces signed a cessation of hostilities agreement, and agreed to start discussions within 6 months. At the same time, the Sudanese Government asked both forces to get out of Sudanese territory. In May 1973, the ELF started a new attack and the civil war was reignited.

- It was under this circumstance the unity of the Eritrean People's Liberation Forces became a reality. The first and second groups were completely united in September 1973 and this unity was joined by that of the Ubel in June of 1974. This united force formally adopted the name Eritrean People's Liberation Forces. The "Forces" in the name was later changed to "Front" at the first EPLF Congress in 1977.

The End of the Civil War

- In the summer of 1974, as some units of the EPLF were moving to the highlands, they faced opposition from ELF units, and the civil war ensued in the highlands. As the civil war that used to take place in remote areas, *now it started* in densely populated area, *and* the public decided to get in between and worked to reconcile

144

the two sides. Forming a reconciliation committee, it proposed a ceasefire, stoppage of blaming each other, and ending the harassment of the supporters of one group by the other group.

- The *position* of the EPLF was: "secondary differences should be resolved through a democratic dialogue". *As a result*, and ever since the beginning of the civil war, it was calling for an end *to the* differences between the different sides of the Eritrean Revolution through dialogue, and *should* focus every military force and effort towards the first enemy, the Ethiopian government. As a result, it accepted the mediation by the public.

- The ELF, on the other hand, rejected the mediation by demanding the EPLF should first go back to Sahel. After this, the ELF launched an attack in Zaghir. After both sides sustained a lot of casualties, the ELF *forces were* pushed towards Mensae. *After the battle of Zaghir, at the end of 1974, due to the pressure of the mass organizations of the ELF on its leadership, together with public opinion, brought an end to the civil war.*

Questions

1. What was the purpose of the Emba Hara Conference, and what was its outcome?

2. What was the reason for the cold relationship between the first and second groups of the EPLF?

3. Briefly explain the effect of Beirut meeting in bringing about the unity of the EPLF.

4. What was the decision of the ELF first National Congress regarding *the* forces that had split from the ELF? What effect did it have on the civil war?

Lesson 32:

The Eritrean Revolution at a Turning Point (1974-1977)

Lesson Goals:

By the end of this lesson, students will gain a basic understanding of the following:

- The role of the Eritrean Revolution in the fall of the Haile Sellasie regime.

- Ethiopian atrocities on Eritrean civilians.

- The flow of tegadelti into the ranks of the liberation armies

- The beginning of unity talks between the EPLF and ELF.

- The break of the Foreign Mission from the EPLF

Eritrean Revolution and the fall of the Haile Sellasie Regime

- In 1973 there was a wide spread famine in Ethiopia that claimed hundreds of thousands of lives. However, the Haile Sellasie regime, in order not to look bad, attempted to hide the famine from the world. This attempt of covering up exacerbated the effects of the famine. When news of this 1973 famine and cover up attempt was exposed to the world it triggered anger among the Ethiopian population.

- In addition to this, an increase in gas price in February of 1974 led to a strike by tax drivers. This strike was joined by students and teachers who had been opposing the monarchy since the 1960s.

- At the same time events in Eritrea made to the people of Ethiopia's courageous opposition to the regime even bolder. The Second Division of the Ethiopian army in Eritrea had a two-week battle against the EPLF and was soundly defeated in Sahel. Angered by this defeat members of the Second Army Division stationed in Eritrea revolted against the regime. This revolt spread to other army members in different parts of Ethiopia. This brought the resignation of the cabinet of ministers led Prime Minister Aklilu Habtewold. After two or three new cabinet of ministers were formed to be later disbanded, Emperor Haile Sellasie was officially deposed on September 1974 and Ethiopia fell under the control of a military regime that called itself the Provisional Military Council or the Dergue.

- With this a popular revolution was hijacked by a military junta that didn't represent it.

- Along with the economic and popular revolt, the Eritrean Revolution was a key factor that pushed the Haile Sellasie regime to its demise.

The Dergue and Governmental Terror

- The uncertain situation in Ethiopia, which was in what one might call revolutionary chaos, together with the ceasefire between the Eritrean liberation fronts created a conducive environment to propel the Eritrean Revolution forward. Eritrean war of independence transitioned from a guerilla hit and run battles to a mobile and stationary battles. With this the Eritrean armed struggle entered a new phase and the support it was getting from the population increased several folds. The Dergue that was paying lip-service to peaceful resolution until it is ready for another offensive, started a new offensive around Asmara in February of 1975 and was soundly defeated.

- The Dergue's secret "Death Squads" started taking young people from their homes in the dark and were strangling them individually and in groups with piano wires and throwing their dead bodies in the streets of Asmara. In addition they started throwing hand grenades into public gatherings. As a result of these acts of terror thousands of innocent civilians were murdered in a short span of time.

- Because the Dergue was killing civilians by the thousands and was looting property, the population in Asmara was completely terrorized. As a result of this chaos (Igirgir in Tigrigna) that came because of the Dergue's terror people started to flee to the country side and Asmara's population dwindled.

- In the other cities, towns and villages, as a continuation of the Haile Sellasie-led scorched earth terror of the 1960s, the Dergue regime was involved in a wide spread of mass murders and burning of villages. Heinous mass murders were committed in Woki-Diba, Umhajer, Hirgigo, Adi Nifas and other places. In 1975 thousands of innocent Eritrean civilians were murdered and maimed en mass. Scored of villages were razed to the ground and hundreds of thousands went into exile and or were internally displaced.

- In June of 1976, the Dergue arming about a hundred thousand poor farmers, launched what it called the Operation "Raza" (Vulture). This army was decimated in a matter of days by the Eritrean Liberation Armies near Zalambesa before it even set foot in Eritrea.

Colonel Mengistu Hailemariam, Chairman of the Ethiopian Military Council (Dergue)

A man who Engineered numerous atrocities against Eritrean civilians

Flow of tegadelti into the Eritrean Revolution

- By the end of 1974, Eritrean youth that had it enough with the Dergue's atrocities on Eritrea's civilians began joining the ranks of Eritrea's freedom fighters in droves from all over the world, but particularly from within Eritrea, the Sudan and Ethiopia. Even members of the Eritrean police force and the Israeli-trained commando forces who had loyally served the Ethiopian regime for many years began joining the two fronts individually and in groups because they couldn't stand the atrocities that were being committed on their own population.

- This new influx of new tegadelti increased the number of tegadelti in the two fronts five to six fold. The number of female tegadelti also increased by many folds.

Flow of young people joining the Liberation Army
A Catalyst for quantitative as well as qualitative change of the Revolution

- This new influx brought not only a numerical change to the ranks of the tegadelti but it also helped the Eritrean Revolution score a qualitative change. Many of these new comers were from the cities and in their ranks were students, workers and professionals. Compared with what was already there this new group had a better level of education, expertise and political maturity and this enabled the Eritrean Revolution to go through a qualitative change.

- The expertise of the new fighter helped bring big change in medicine, education, transportation, maintenance, administration and other areas. As a result of all these, and by developing its military power, the Eritrean Revolution was able to tip the balance of power in its favor.

The Issue of Unity and the Breaking of the Foreign Mission from the EPLF

- After the ceasefire, tegadelti of the ELF and EPLF began having unofficial contacts and dialogue among themselves. In addition to these the leadership of the two fronts were also talking with each other to coordinate military operations.

- In March of 1975 rapprochement committees were formed to centralize the unofficial contacts that were going on between the tegadelti of the two fronts.

- Under these circumstances the ELF held its second congress in May of 1975. The congress came out with a new political program. It resolved to initiate dialogue with the EPLF to with the aim of establish a single National Democratic Organization in Eritrea. The Congress elected a 41-member Revolutionary Council. The Revolutionary Council on its part elected a 9-member Executive Committee with Ahmed Naser as the Chair and Ibrahim Totil as a Vice-Chair.

- The new ELF leadership announced that it had established a Rapprochement Committee with members from the rank and file as well as leaders of the organization. This ELF Rapprochement Committee, began talks with the Foreign Mission of the EPLF lead by Osman Saleh Sabe bypassing the EPLF leadership in the field and ignoring the ongoing rapprochement contacts. Both sides met in Khartoum in September 1975 and signed a hasty unity agreement.

- On 11 November 1975, the EPLF tegadelti held what is called the first Semienawi-Bahri Conference and rejected the Khartoum Unity Agreement that was signed between the ELF and the Foreign Mission without the knowledge of the EPLF leadership in the field. Instead showing its willingness for talks, elected a new Rapprochement Committee.

- Sabe's reaction to this was in March of 1976 he announced that he along with his few followers inside and outside Eritrea had broken away from the EPLF and forming a new organization called the ELF-PF.

Questions

1. Explain the role of the Eritrean Revolution in the demise of the Haile Sellasie regime.
2. List the qualitative change brought into the Revolution by those who joined in the mid 1970s.
3. What was the reason for the split between the EPLF and Sabe's Foreign Mission.

Lesson 33:

First Organizational Congress of the Eritrean People's Liberation Forces

---

Lesson Goals:

At the end of this lesson; students are expected to gain basic knowledge about the following points:

- The organizational and national importance of the first congress of the Eritrean People's Liberation Forces

- The National Democratic Political Program and its political, military and socio–economic policies.

- The EPLF carried out its first organizational congress in January 1977 at Fah, Sahel. About 300 representatives of tegadelti (combatants) and civilians, delegates from six nations, representatives of Liberation movements and progressive parties from neighboring countries and the world attended the Congress. The Congress deliberated and evaluated political, economic, social and military issues and came up with clear resolutions for the organization and approved the National Democratic Program, new organizational structure and elected its leaders.

The Eritrean People's Liberation Forces First Congress

- Based on the newly approved organizational structure, the Congress elected thirty seven permanent and six alternate members of the Central Committee. In addition an eleven-member Politburo with Romodan Mohammed Nur as the Secretary General and Isaias Afwerki as Vice Secretary General were elected.

- The major achievement of the first Organizational Congress is the approval of the National Democratic Program. The program worked as a road map for the national democratic struggle to achieve national independence, justice and democracy. Some of the major goals of the National Democratic program were:

  1. Establish People's Democratic Government
  2. Establish a planned national economy based on the principles of Self-reliance and independent of external intervention.
  3. Modernize culture, education, vocational skills and health services
  4. Guarantee the rights of workers , women, and nationals in need of social support
  5. Strength and safeguard the equality and unity of ethnic groups
  6. Establish a strong people's army and follow the strategy of *people's war*.
  7. Safeguard freedom of religion and belief
  8. Follow a peaceful and non-aligned foreign policy

- In general the program was a revolutionary national political program aimed at achieving a national independence and making fundamental changes to adjust the socio economic and political inequities among the Eritrean population and to eventually establish a democratic political system.

- The congress changed the name "Eritrean people's liberation Forces" to "Eritrean People's Liberation Front" and approved the

154

design of the EPLF's flag and emblem. It established a monthly publication titled "Merih" that states the vision of the organization and decided "Victory to the masses" to be the slogan of the organization.

Romedan Mohammed Nur, EPLF Secretary General 1977 - 1987

- On issues related to national unity, the Congress considered the complete unity of Eritrean organizations as its strategic goal. The congress believed that the best way to achieve the goal is through establishing a United Front. On military issues, the congress stated and believed that liberating land step by step as the best option and recommended it continues. The congress drew three military strategies:

    1. **Positional Warfare:** Defending the liberated areas, destroying enemy military bases and liberate the land and people step by step

    2. **Mobile Warfare:** To carry out attacks in the semi-liberated areas to prevent free enemy mobility

155

3. **Guerrilla Warfare**: To attack and destroy fuel depots, armament stores, economic and military bases of the enemy on areas under the complete control of the enemy.

Questions

1. Explain the importance of the first organizational congress of the EPLF.
2. State five goals from the first National Democratic Program.
3. Explain the differences between positional, mobile and guerrilla warfares.

Lesson 34:

Eritrean Revolution and the Liberation of Towns

Lesson Goals:

At the end of this lesson; students are expected to gain basic knowledge about the following points:

- The conditions that contributed to the acceleration of the revolution and the success of the liberation of towns

- The socio-economic and political changes and goals the revolution initiated,

- The efforts towards unity

Beloved Eritrea, the towns have become our bases
Trumpet of victory is sounding already
The enemy's base at Afabet is in flames
Its outposts swept away from Sahel
Gallant tegadelti are bearing good news to the masses
Our selfless heroes are attacking like a lightening
Giving themselves for their beloved country

- We have seen that after 1975, the military balance of power had started to tip in favor of the Eritrean Revolution. As a result, by 1976, 90% of Eritrea's rural areas were under the control of the Eritrean Revolution. The resolution of the first national organizational congress strategy to purse a peoples' war to liberate land and people step by step had good outcome, and was proven correct and was decided to continue with it. After the Congress, the peoples' army had shown spontaneous progress. The Ethiopian

157

army was pushed from many strategic places of Eritrea and ended up encircled in few towns.

- Karora was the first town that lead the way for towns to be liberated. It was under the control of the people's army by the beginning of January 1977. Nakfa was the second town to liberated in March 1977 after a siege of nearly six months. The Ethiopian army had mobilized its forces from Keren to save it, but was destroyed in the Anseba River and another airborne attempt by helicopters was destroyed in the Rora plains. In the process of liberating towns, Nakfa depicted change of the Eritrean Revolution towards strategic offensive and had a symbolic and substantive role.

- The people's army continued its progress and liberated Afabet on the 6th of April 1977, two weeks after the liberation of Nakfa. The Ethiopian army was shocked and was forced to withdraw from its smaller bases and concentrated it forces in defense of the bigger towns.

- The number of new recruits to the ranks of the Eritrean Revolution rose in mid-1970's and it drastically boosted the number and status of the military units. By this time the people's army was organized by brigades. After this new reorganization, the peoples' liberation army simultaneously attacked Dekemhare and Keren liberating them on July 1977. After these Segeneiti and Digsa were also liberated. The dynamics of victory continued. By the end of 1977, the city of Asmara was fully encircled. Ghindae and the entire road from Asmara to Massawa was liberated. More than half of Massawa was also under the control of the people's army.

- In 1977, the ELF on its part liberated Omhajer, Tessenei, Adi-Quala, Mendefera and Akordet. This implies that at of the beginning of 1978, except for Assab, Asmara, Adi-Keih, Barentu and a part of Massawa, almost all of Eritrea was liberated. There was high expectation by the people for the complete liberation of Eritrea.

SOCIO-ECONOMIC CHANGES INITIATED BY THE REVOLUTION

In 1977, along with the ever growing liberated area, the Eritrean Revolution started to implement its socio economic and political programs. To mention the major ones:

1. Land Tenure system

The traditional land tenure system had left many poor farmers, households and especially women without access to land. As a result efforts were made to equitably allocate land to all residents.

2. Health service

- After 1975, hundreds of medical professionals joined the Eritrean Revolution and the provision of health services increased in quantity and quality. Beside tegadelti, the general public started to benefit. New hospitals and clinics were established. Medical services, using mobile medical units and foot doctors, were provided for citizens living in remote rural areas.

- After the strategic withdrawal of 1978 especially during the 1980s, the EPLF was able to expand and develop its medical services. The EPLF had the Orota central hospital, together with other hospitals and clinics and front line medical operation units providing medical services to the army and general public. At this stage the health services in the field was getting world recognition.

- The health department established a center that trained thousands of lower and medium level medical professionals, set up a factory that produced variety of basic medicines, printed books and magazines to disseminate health-related knowledge and information.
- The ELF for its part had established medium and big health facilities in the liberated areas and was providing medical services to the tegadelti and the general public.

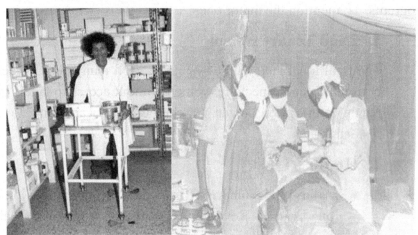

A pharmacy in the Liberated areas   Doctors Performing Surgery in the Liberated Areas

3. Education

- Eradicating illiteracy was given a top priority and the effort done in the mid 1970s substantially reduced illiteracy among the tegadelti.

- In 1975 – 76, the EPLF and ELF prepared national curriculum and started to print books for the elementary and junior level. Schools were opened in the liberated rural areas and then in the liberated towns. The Revolution school was the main and biggest school in the liberated areas; thousands of students were the beneficiaries. At the end of 1977, the ELF opened "TSIBAH" school and many benefited from it.

- The CAMPAIGN TO ERADICATE ILLITERACY that started in 1983 in the liberated and semi liberated areas was an important program for the civilians.

- Books were available to provide education and skill training on all fields of activities: military, technical, construction, agriculture etc. As a result, thousands of nationals gained skill training.

Tegadelti Attending Classes

4. Public responsibility

- The EPLF's fundamental belief was in the increasing of the political awareness, organizing and arming the public. "Hafash ynkah, *ywedeb*, yteatek" (let the masses get aware, organized and armed) was its slogan. The EPLF was strongly convinced that victory could not be achieved without increasing the political awareness, organizing and arming the general public. The population was organized in different public associations, and peoples' militia and regional armies were established.

- At the end of 1970s, National union of women, farmers, workers, students and youth were established. These unions played crucial role in overcoming the divisive and narrow sub-nationalist feelings of the population, raising the political awareness on national unity and the participation of the public in the Eritrean Revolution.

- For the public to be actively involved on administrative issues, vestiges of traditional and colonial administration had to be abolished and replaced with Eritrean public administrations. In the liberated and semi-liberated areas, people's assemblies and associations were formed through elections. Bidho (Defense) Committees were also formed.

Women's Participation

- "No revolution succeeds without women's participation" was one of the fundamental beliefs of the EPLF. To this end tremendous efforts were made to raise the political awareness of women, overcome traditional norms and beliefs that hindered women from active participation, and eventually were organized and armed so as to be the pillar for Eritrean Revolution. The Eritrean women achieved their right and equality through their heroic sacrifices. It was a great leap forward for the role played by the Eritrean women.

- The EPLF had a strong conviction and worked indefatigable for women's equal rights marriage, divorce, inheritance, land ownership rights, political participation, education and skills-training etc. The EPLF waged a struggle against traditional cultural norms and male chauvinism that undermined and oppressed women.

- The Eritrean women had a slogan "Equality through practical participation" and implemented it. The Eritrean women heroic participation in the history of the liberation struggle was

162

exemplary. The limited number of women tegadelti in the 1970s showed substantial increase in the 1980s and reached up to 35%; that meant thousands in number. The breakdown by sector is shown below:

Description	Women participation in %
1. Combatant	23.0
2. Industry	29.5
3. Transport	25.9
4. Health	55.2
5. Construction	19.6
6. Agriculture	19.8
7. Electronics	25.0
8. National program (education, culture, news, social activities etc	17.4
9. Finance	9.5
10. Communication	33.1

*Table showing **women participation in the struggle by sector (1989)***

- Women participation was not limited to tegadelti in the liberation struggle. Hundreds of thousands of women living in the liberated and semi-liberated areas, cities and surrounding areas under enemy occupation and women living abroad were dedicated members of mass organizations and their contributions were immense and crucial.

Women Tegadelti in Battle **Women Tegadelti Working as News Broadcasters**

Public Associations/organizations

- The establishment and strengthening of public associations and the replacement of old organizations' were helpful to counter sub-nationalist feelings that persisted in the Eritrean public. Starting in 1979, congresses were organized for the establishment of the National Union of Eritrean women, the National Union of Eritrean workers and the National Union of Eritrean students.

- These association played crucial role in the liberation struggle by organizing the masses and raising political awareness. Many members of these associations joined the armed struggle and they made material and financial contributions. In addition to the stated associations, the Eritrean Medical Association was also established.

- The Eritrean Relief Association (ERA) was established in 1975 and it did a marvelous work in getting and disbursing assistance to drought and war affected citizens. During the 1984/85 worst famine in Eritrea and Ethiopia, ERA played a paramount role in distributing emergency food aid to people living in the liberated and semi liberated areas.

Emergency Relief Supply by ERA

Effort for unity: achievements and failures

- The civil war that started in 1972 stopped in 1974 mainly for the following reasons:

    1. The inability of the ELF to liquidate the EPLF by force

    2. Rejection of civil war by the nationalist and democratic tegadelti of the ELF

    3. The Eritrean public's call for unity and resolute stand against the civil war.

    4. The opportunity created by the overthrow of the Haile Sellasie regime

- When the civil war lapsed, the leaders of the EPLF and the ELF residing in the high lands of Eritrea started to meet in order to coordinate military operations against the enemy. At the same time meetings were taking place among tegadelti of the two organizations for the purpose of unity. As a continuation, on March 1975 liaison committees were established to organize tegadelti' meetings. However, the meeting was temporarily stopped since the ELF was planning to organize its Second National Congress on May of 1975.

- As the situation continued, an EPLF foreign affairs official visited the field on May 1975 to observe and discuss developments. The visiting dignitary was briefed on the development on the process of unity and for the EPLF liaison committee was waiting for the ELF liaison committee to finish its congress.

- The ELF completed its second organizational congress in May. The Congress officially ordered a stop to the already halted civil war and mandated a restarting of negotiations with the EPLF. The Congress elected new leaders and these leaders appointed new liaison committee to carry on with the negotiations. The newly elected ELF liaison committee instead of meeting with the already appointed liaison committee of the EPLF, it traveled abroad to meet with the EPLF Foreign Mission. The ELF liaison committee met with the Foreign Mission official of the EPLF in Khartoum in September 1975 and the two stated their decision to facilitate unity. The EPLF held a conference for the representatives of the tegadelti inside Eritrea on November 12, 1975, at Semenawi Bahri and stated its rejection of the Khartoum agreement and appointed a new liaison committee to restart the negotiations.

- On March 25, 1976, the Foreign Mission declared its decision to split from the EPLF and forming a third new organization named "ELF-PLF" (Eritrean Liberation Front-People's Liberation Forces).

- For this reason and other obstacles the negotiations for unity faced hurdles for some time. At the end of 1976, a civilian liaison committee was formed with the task of bringing the two organizations for unity discussions. After several subsequent meetings, a meeting of the population was organized in TSEBELA attended by 350 peoples' representatives from many parts of the country and the meeting called for the unity of both organizations. This people's initiative shows clearly the active participation of the citizens on issues of the struggle.

- This people's initiative and pressure from friendly countries resulted in the signing of the Unity agreement on October 20, 1977. These agreement known as the Khartoum declaration stated as:
    1. Unity to be achieved through joint works and unification process
    2. The need to form a joint committee consisting of top political leaders to coordinate the works of the two organizations.
    3. Plan joint military strategy; establish different committees to function under the top political leaders in order to coordinate the work of the different departments of the organizations.

Questions
1. State the reasons why the military balance of power shifted towards the Eritrean Revolution after 1975?
2. What was the significance of the liberation of Nakfa?
3. List the towns liberated by the Eritrean Revolution in 1977/78?
4. State the socio economic and political changes as the result of the revolution?
5. Explain the developments that led to the agreement of October 20?

Lesson 35:

Question and Discussion Period

Discussion in groups

- Every classroom forms groups, with each group electing a chairperson and secretary and discussing on assigned topics. A summary of the discussion is then presented to the class.
- Assuming a period is 60 minutes long, 25 minutes are allocated for the discussion part and the remaining 35 minutes for the group presentations.

Points for discussion (to be answered in groups):

1. Discuss the work performed parallel with the armed struggle to bring up socio economic changes and its role to achieve victory for the military liberation struggle by the Eritrean people.

2. The civil war was a continuation of the divisive and exclusionary political stand. Discuss.

3. The Ethiopian atrocities in the Eritrean cities of 1975-76 and the chaos that ensued commonly referred to as "Igirgir" is vivid in the Eritrean collective memory. Discuss about this time from what you have heard from people you know.

4. What is the meaning when we say "The National Democratic Revolution is a multifaceted revolution"? Discuss.

Lesson 36:

Change in the balance of military power and strategic withdrawal

---

Lesson Goals

At the end of this lesson; students are expected to gain knowledge about the following points:

- The Soviet Union's intervention on the side of the Ethiopian Military regime (Dergue) and the subsequent change in the military balance of power

- Consecutive Ethiopian military offensives against the Eritrean Revolution

- Meaning and process of the strategic withdrawal

THE SOVIET UNION'S INTERVENTION ON THE SIDE OF DERGUE

- After the Second World War and the beginning of the "cold war" the regime of Haile Sellasie had allied itself with the western camp which was lead by the United States of America. As a result the Ethiopian regime was provided with an all-round of political, diplomatic, military and economic assistance. Until June 1974, the total economic and military assistance given to Ethiopia by the United State of America was higher than the sum total of assistance given to all sub-Saharan African countries.

- The Haile Sellasie regime, on its part sent Ethiopian troops to South Korea to fight alongside the USA and it also gave the Kagnew military base that served the USA for intelligence and other purposes. This US-Ethiopia cooperation lasted up to 1974. After the overthrow of Haile Sellasie by Dergue military junta, the above economic relationship drastically declined until it was finally cut off in July 1977.

- The Dergue Military regime soon allied itself with the Socialist Camp and in particular with the Soviet Union, so as to have an alternative supply of military assistance.

- The Soviet Union on its part was looking for an ally in the "Horn of Africa" to accomplish its national interest, and it never hesitated to cooperate. As a result of this cooperation, the intervention of the Soviet Union began and it paved the way for prolonged political and economic pressure and suffering of the Eritrean people and the region for a much longer period. As an illustration of these, the Soviet Union equipped the Dergue with weapons worth 1 to 2 billion US dollars from 1977 – 1978. There were also 12,000 Cuban troops and 1,500 senior Russian Military advisors.

- In such a critical circumstance, the EPLF had only two alternatives: one was to defend the already liberated cities and towns at enormous human and material costs overstretching itself and fighting an unbalanced war or withdrawing in an orderly way along with weapons and properties in tact to a remote but reliable and defensible base.

- The first alternative was not feasible with the political and military realities of the time. Therefore, the Eritrean Revolution chose the second alternative; that of strategic withdrawal. It must be emphasized that the strategic withdrawal was not a result of "hopelessness" or "defeatism". The purpose of the strategic withdrawal was to keep intact the peoples' army and weaponry, move to a defensive and strong position, put the enemy force into a protracted war, (war of attrition) and ultimately win the armed struggle.

- The strategic withdrawal was carried out by keeping the human capabilities and armament intact and at the same time inflicting heavy losses on the enemy. The war at Elabered and Maamide were good examples where big military victories were achieved. Because of the strategic withdrawal, thousands of civilians were displaced and had to take refuge in the liberated area and the EPLF completed its strategic withdrawal while taking care and defending the displaced civilians from the enemy.

The Dergue's Successive military offensive against the Eritrean Revolution

- Between June 1978 and December 1983 the Ethiopian colonial army launched seven massive and successive military offensives against the Eritrean Revolution. Soon after the beginning of strategic withdrawal in mid July of 1978, the "FIRST MILITARY OFFENSIVE" continued uninterrupted until the end of August. As a consequence, EPLF trenches on the southern and northern parts of Asmara, near the vicinity of Emba Derho were vacated.

- The Second Offensive began on the 20th of November 1978 and lasted up to the end of the month. As a consequence, the EPLF vacated its defensive positions from the eastern and southern sides of Keren.

- The Third offensive lasted from January up to February 9th 1979 and was carried out in Anseba, Maamide, and Northern Sahel and around Denden (east of Nakfa).

- The fourth offensive lasted from March 30th up to April 11th 1979. This failed military campaign was aimed at breaking the Northern Sahel and Nakfa fronts.

- The Eritrean Revolution not only succeeded in defending and averting the defeat of the revolution, but it managed to carry out effective and an important counter offensive behind enemy lines.

- After all these continuous and intense military offensives, the Dergue made additional military preparations and carried out the fifth military offensive that lasted between July 8, 1979 up to end of the month. However, similar to the preceding offensives, this military offensive as well was foiled with a heavy loss of about 12,000 enemy troops and numerous military armaments.

- After the subsequent defeats, the Eritrean Revolution gained morale and material strength and decided to shift from defensive toward offensive strategy. Based on this decision, massive offensives were carried out on the beginning of December 1979 and another supportive counter offensive in Northern Sahel.

- In these offensives, the Ethiopian army lost 15,000 soldiers. The enemy garrisoned in the northern Sahel was confined to the flat areas. The enemy garrisoned in the Nakfa area retreated back to Afabet. These military offensives had more political impact than military. The perception after the strategic withdrawal was that the complete annihilation of the Eritrean Revolution. These victorious offensives confirmed that the EPLF had prevailed militarily and as a result the moral of the enemy started to decline.

- After the strategic withdrawal and five consecutive massive offensives and subsequent counter offensives by the EPLF, the Ethiopian army had a huge setback in terms of material and human losses. The human loss reached 52,000 troops killed and wounded.

This occurred while the military balance of power was still in favor of the enemy and it was a huge victory for the Eritrean Revolution.

Questions

1. What were the basic factors for the cooperation of the Dergue regime and the Soviet Union?
2. State the military assistance given in mid 1978 that reflect the massive intervention of the Soviet Union?
3. Elaborate the counter measures taken by the Eritrean Revolution against the successive military offensives of the Dergue regime?

Lesson 37:

The reigniting of the civil war and the subsequent disintegration of the ELF.

Lesson Goals:

At the end of this lesson; students are expected to gain knowledge about the following points:

- o The causes for the beginning of the second bloody civil war
- o The progress and outcome of the factional fighting
- o The disintegration of the ELF

- After the agreement reached by the EPLF and ELF on October 20th, 1977 they started to meet in April 1978 to discuss its practical interpretation. These initial discussions led to the two organizations to realistically implement and subsequently achieve complete cooperation and coordination by having a joint senior political leadership, joint military, information, economy as well as establishing joint committees on social issues and foreign affairs. Soon after, the most senior political leaders held meetings from 1979 up to 1980, with the objective of implementing the agreements and fulfill the complete unity of the two organizations.

- Contrary to the above agreements that gave hope and cooperation of the two organizations, there were many unsolved obstacles that caused serious breakup of relationships.

- Beginning of mid 1980, the relationship of the two organizations declined from bad to worse. On June 6th, 1980, some military units of the ELF attacked the EPLF military unit stationed near the

174

village of Engel in Northern Dankalia and forced them to evacuate the area.

- Another coincidence that led to the highest confrontation was the withdrawal of the two military brigades of the ELF stationed in the northern Sahel Front along with the EPLF. The unexpected withdrawal happened on July 1980 without informing the EPLF.

- After the withdrawal of the two brigades of ELF from the Northern Sahel Front, the conflict reached its climax and a point of no return. Soon after, the civil war was reignited.

- Even though all the above stated reasons could directly be considered as the major causes of the civil war, the ultimate and most decisive cause could exclusively be attributed to the anti-unity faction within the top leadership of the ELF.

- While the civil war was raging on, the "Arab League" invited a meeting in Tunis, (the capital of Tunisia) with the agenda of restarting peaceful negotiations and ultimately uniting the two organizations. In the Tunis meeting, resolutions were passed to stop the civil war, halt blackmailing propaganda and form a committee that follows the unity of the organizations. However, all the efforts could not stop the civil war and it continued. Finally, in August 1981 the military forces of the ELF were pushed over to the sovereign territory of the Republic of the Sudan. As soon as they crossed the border, the Sudanese government disarmed them.

- The ELF in the Sudan was divided into several antagonistic factions with irreconcilable opinions. As a result, it was the end of ELF existences as a unified organization in Eritrea.

THE DISINTEGRATION OF THE ELF

- Although its military conflict with the EPLF facilitated its downfall, the serious internal contradictions of the ELF were the decisive factors for its total disintegration.

- The deep rooted differences and friction in the ELF leadership had manifested itself on different occasions. In 1976, however, a faction of the ELF nicknamed "Fallul" (anarchists) rejected the top leadership of the ELF, reached a critical stage. Since its inception, there were competition and frictions that resulted in the creation of new factions such as "Islamic", "labor party" "rightist" and also "Baathist" factions, and others. As a result of these and the formation of a dominant, reactionary and divisive power were the two major causes for the disintegration of the organization.

- The prevailing internal contradictions and differences reached to a point of no return when the ELF was pushed into the Sudan. For such reasons, the organization disintegrated into different units with diverse political poles.

Questions

1. Mention the causes for the resurgent civil war?
2. Explain the outcome of the resurgent civil war?

Lesson 38:
SAHEL, THE MAIN DEFENSIVE MILITARY BASE OF THE REVOLUTION

Lesson Goals:

At the end of this lesson; students are expected to gain knowledge about the following points:

- The meaning and importance of defensive military base
- Activities carried out in the defensive military base

Revolutionary Sahel, our base
Is the launching pad to all corners of Eritrea
Mountains of Sahel, our base
Is the launching pad to all corners of Eritrea

In the 1970s at the birth of the EPLF
When it was an infant before was able to walk
Our base Sahel, our pride
Was the basis for the future of Eritrea

Plains, vallies, rocks and mountains
Inpenteratable rivers and hills
Fruit of hard work
Networks to all fronts
The plains of Qetan the Garrage at Aget
The valley at Debaat refugee center
Seberqete-Zagre steep mountains
Zero-Blieqat educational base
Historic Fah, source of news, hub of all activities.

Gurieto-Algien, Wedgan of red soil
Maamide-Azhara, the river of Qebrwe't

Illa Saeda-Tigih, the peaks of Shiglet
The strategic Arag, plains of Halibet
In the process of the struggle

Mountains of Sahel, our base
Is the launching pad to all corners of Eritrea
Eritrean Yanan, our base
Is the launching pad to all corners of Eritrea

Amberbeb-Tsabra, Nakfa the strategic place
The Gelil passage-Hiday, entry point to Afabet
Strong trenches

The bastion of the oppressed unparalleled in our history
Unfazed by the hubris of the arrogant
Has annihilated every offensive that came its way
Let's remember the past, the struggle
enemy corps at Naro.

Let's remember it in the struggle
How it buried Haile Sellasie's hubris
How it smashed the yoke of colonialism
The opportunistic trap of the destructive movement
Still it is waiting ready with a grave to bury the Dergue

Sahel our base, the strong trench
It trains and builds our gallant army
It archives and collects all our handi works
No body will threaten it, the base of our Revolution
The core of political awareness
Guarantor of victory, Sahel, the bastion of the oppressed

It is over you cowards
Illaberid-Tsebab, Nakfa and Maamide
Felket and Aget that brought justice
What did your satellite messaging send
The Dergue and its advisors, the generals,
They met the recipe of their dreams

This is the strategy of a peoples' war
It knows no rush, never in a hurry
Guerilla, mobile warfare to whip the arrogant
For the continuation of the Revolution
To defend the oppressed
Starting from Sahel
We will liberate our population

- The massive intervention of the Soviet Union definitely interrupted the Eritrean Revolution. Thus, under the circumstances where the balance of military power was in favor of Ethiopia, the only alternative for the EPLF, in order to come out victorious in the long run, was to implement the strategy of protracted people's war. In the process of the prolonged war, the revolution armed the people; followed the core principles of self-reliance, and had to put in place economic foundations that support the war of liberation. To implement such plans, there was a need for a defensible and secure base area.

Map showing Revolution's Base at Sahel

- When we say "permanent base", we mean all the areas in the front line, as well as the trenches of the EPLA. This area extended from northern Sahel all the way to Nakfa up to Hal Hal. It has to be mentioned that Arag, Anberbeb, Himbol, and Arareb were the most secure base areas of the EPLF. In addition, the units who operate behind enemy lines, (mobile units and guerrilla fighters) had their own tactical bases.

- The Command Center of the EPLF's top leadership, Radio station (voice of the broad masses of Eritrea) and various offices and departments were stationed in the base area in Sahel. All major works that laid down the foundation for future economic development of Eritrea were carried out in the base area in Sahel. The socio-economic development that had began with the liberation of cities in the mid 1970s had shown refined qualitative changes. Efforts were made to establish different social organizations with the ultimate goal for the people to help each other and create the culture of team work. To mention some activities carried out in the base area were: arms depot, health services, logistics, transport, small scale factories, schools, cultural activities, news services, support for the war-disabled, child care and orphanages. To have better understanding, we state the following examples:

CONSTRUCTION

- The base was the place where all economic activities began and the Construction of roads was given priority. Roads were built in the mountainous and difficult terrain of Sahel. In addition, many networks of roads were built to interlink the liberated and semi-liberated areas.

- According to the official report of the Department of Construction of the EPLF, a total of 1,000 Kilometer long roads were built.

180

Taking into consideration the construction technology adopted, the roads built testify and reflect the engineering skill of that time. One of the impressive roads built during the armed struggle was the 12-kilometer road called "Biddho" (Challenge) Road.

The Biddho Road in Sahel

- A lot of effort was spent to facilitate the construction works underway in the base area and to fulfill the high construction demands. As a result of the experience that was gained, the construction capability of the EPLF was improved, residential houses, stores, schools, health centers, garages, buildings for small scale industries, small dams, diversion canals and houses for the displaced people were constructed. Bricks and other construction materials were produced to satisfy the high demand at the base area. To have qualified skilled manpower, training for construction workers was organized.

TRANSPORT

- The transport vehicles captured from the enemy were the foundation for the EPLF Department of Transport. More work needed to be done to expand and guarantee for sustainable utilization. To make best use of available resources, the EPLF established and expanded the transport unit and garages and started to produce tires and car batteries and other consumables in the base area.

MANUFACTURING

- Producing basic consumable items and tools were the goal of the economic activities carried out in the EPLF base area. For this reason, workshops and small scale industries were established. The established manufacturing industries were those of: plastic sandals, sanitary napkins, packed food stuff, flour mills, kitchen utensils, wood and metal workshops to produce construction and household items, Pasta factories, bakeries, leather products and tailoring workshop, as well as electrical workshops were established.

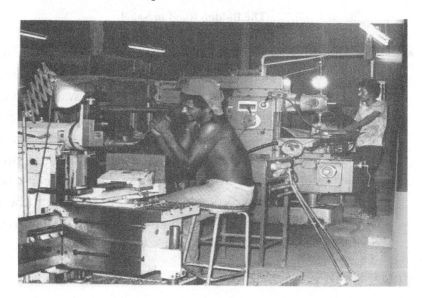

One of the Metal Workshops in Sahel

INFORMATION, mass media

- Information (mass media) was crucial to increase public political awareness and the peoples' participation in the liberation struggle. The EPLF from its inception had good perception about the importance of mass media and was disseminating news through different mechanisms. The liberation of towns was a good opportunity for the people and the organization to have contacts. The situation changed after the strategic withdrawal of the EPLF. There had to be an alternative for the people to get timely and up to date information. It was, therefore, for this purpose that the EPLF established the Radio station of the Voice of the broad masses of Eritrea on the 1st of January 1979 at "fah", Sahel. The radio station played a crucial role in broadcasting true information about the Eritrean armed struggle until the liberation on May 24th 1991. In addition, the EPLF established printing press, photographic and video studios.

HEALTH

- In the base area: several hospitals were built and expanded. In the liberated and semi liberated areas, fixed, mobile clinics and units of "foot doctors" increased in number. To increase the number of medical staff, training for mid-wives and other medical personnel were provided.

- The Department of Health of the EPLF was convinced on the importance of producing essential medicines locally. A pharmaceutical was established and started producing infusion, penicillin, sulphonamides, tetracycline, aspirin, chloroquine (to cure malaria), vitamin–c, anti TB medicine, syrups and other ointments. The number of people getting medical service increased from time to time and as of 1986, the beneficiaries reached 880,000.

EDUCATION

- In the base area, the liberated and semi-liberated areas and refugee camps, efforts were made to establish elementary schools and junior high schools. Providing basic academic education was not enough and for this reason, the EPLF opened the technical school in 1985 to give training on various technical skills. Besides, intensive works were carried out in developing curriculum, preparation of teaching materials and training qualified teachers and construction of schools.

Students Attending Class at the Revolution School

SOCIAL SERVICES

- Rehabilitation centers for drought and war displaced citizens, centers for thousands of displaced families and orphans (known as "Enda Hizbi") were established in the base area. The centers were used as a safe heaven, rehabilitation and recovery. For the War Disabled Veterans, the Biddho Rehab Center (Medeber Senkulan Biddho) was established.

ETHIOPIAN PRISONERS OF WAR (POWs)

- The EPLF had a clear policy regarding prisoners of war. With its meager resources, the EPLF was treating the POW humanely, provided them with adequate food, shelter, clothing, medical and educational services. On several occasions, the EPLF freed the POW but the Dergue was bringing them back to war and for this reason, the EPLF had no alternative but to let the freed POWs' live a normal life inside the base area.
- Substantial numbers of the POWs were convinced and believed on the just cause of the Eritrean people for independence and joined the EPLF and Ethiopian opposition organizations. In the life time of the armed struggle of the Eritrean people, about 140,000 to 150,000 Ethiopian troops were captured. Out of the total POWs, about 100,000 were captured during the last phase of the war of independence.

Questions

1. What does a base area mean?
2. Mention some activities that were carried out in the base area?

Lesson 39:

Sixth Offensive: Exemplary challenge and determination

Lesson Goals:

At the end of this lesson; students are expected to gain knowledge about the following points:

- Political, Diplomatic and Military preparation of the Dergue for its sixth offensive

- The EPLF and the broad masses of Eritrea's stand against the offensive

- The process and outcome of sixth offensive

- The Stealth Offensive "Selahta Werar"

I Dare you, I Dare you, I Dare you

A 19 year old revolution
You are attempting to destroy by force
I Dare you, I Dare you
I am ready for your next offensive

Let them pile up arms by the plane load
Let them mobilize armies, airborne and infantry
Let advisors flow, leaders of offensives
Neither will I bend nor bow down
I will never kneel down
I Dare you, I Dare you
My stand is clear ready till death and the grave

186

Let them drench my land with suffocating poison
Let them spray my body with poison gas
Let them use chemical warfare
The unity of my people
The justness of my cause
Would not change a bit
By barbaric fascistic chemical warfare

- The sixth offensive, also called as "Red Star Campaign" by the Dergue was the largest, fiercest and challenging of all the previous successive offensives that aimed to destroy and exterminate the EPLF. It has already been mentioned that the Dergue had carried out five offensives to destroy the Eritrean Revolution. The unique thing about the sixth offensive was that it took two solid years for the Dergue to make diplomatic, political, economic and propaganda preparations. The massive preparation for the offensive and during the start of the operation, the offensive was also stated as a *panacea for Eritrean problem.* Just to mentions some of the preparations:

  o The Dergue carried out intensive diplomatic campaigns with the intension to convince and stop foreign sympathizers and supporters from supporting the Eritrean Revolution. As a result, at the beginning of the summer of 1981, the governments of South Yemen, Mohamed Gaddafi of Libya and Ethiopia signed joint military defense pact. Immediately after that Libya provided Ethiopia with an assistance of US $250 Million. President Jaafer Numeiri of the Republic of the Sudan completely stoped sympathizing with the Eritrean Revolution, closed all Eritrean functions carried out in the Sudan, cut off all activities crossing to Eritrea through the Sudanese border. More than any time the Eritrean Revolution was isolated and encircled.

187

- The Dergue regime had done lot of work to isolate the Eritrean Revolution from its own people and make the "Red Star Campaign" look like it had been supported by the Eritrean people. The Dergue officially made false promise to implement development projects for the benefit of Eritrean people.

- The Dergue's pretentious act was to reduce illegal imprisonment and disappearance. More festivals, seminars and political meetings were organized in many places.

- In the Military apparatus, the Dergue was able to have 120,000 well armed troops and that was one of the biggest modern army in black Africa. Out of the total number of troops, 50,000 troops; named as **Mountain Army,** were well trained to fight in mountainous terrain. In general, the military preparation of the Dergue regime were as follows:

  - 15 divisions of ground troops
  - 2 mechanized brigades
  - 8 battalions armed with tanks
  - 16 artillery battalions
  - 5 anti aircraft units
  - 4 ballistic missile units
  - 200 brand new tanks
  - 500 heavy trucks
  - 124 modern helicopters (24 of them are MI-24, sophisticated helicopters gunships).

- The Soviet Union sent four Army Generals to plan and lead the war, and the number of Soviet military advisors was increased in number and expertise.

- Another unique military development was the obsession of the Dergue military regime to completely wipe out the Eritrean Revolution by using poison gas, violating all international laws and agreements.

Preparation by the Eritrean Revolution and the people

The preparations by the EPLF were:

- National declaration of mobilization so that the masses would contribute whatever they can to fend off the offensive

- Strengthen its defenses to minimize causalities

- Set up temporary medical operating stations

- Carry out widespread seminars to raise the morale of the public and tegadelti

- Distributed Atropine syringes; anti poison gas, to the tegadelti and gas masks were prepared

- The EPLF was organized in 10 brigades. From all units, additional 3 Battalions were formed and all able tegadelti stationed in the base area were assigned to the front line. All in all, the total number of fighting force were not more than 13,000. This meant that the military balance of power was based on the ratio of 1 freedom fighter against 10 Ethiopian troops. Besides the slogan of the EPLF of the day was "no matter how big the invading army, it will be consumed by flame of the revolution." This slogan raised the morale and psyche of the tegadelti and the Eritrean people.

189

Ethiopia's Arsenal for the 6th Offensive Tegadelti Ready with Improvised Gas Masks for Chemical Warfare

The offensive

- After two years of massive preparations, Mengistu Hailemariam and all his cabinet Ministers came to Asmara to lead and closely monitor the progress. The war began on February 15th, 1982 and continued uninterrupted for 95 days (i.e. over three months). The offensive began from three fronts namely:
    1. The North Eastern Sahel Front
    2. The Nakfa Front
    3. The Barka and Halhal Fronts
- On the 15th of February (the day the offensive started) it was the 21st military division, that opened the war from Koken, Barka and was immediately repulsed by the EPLF. In the fighting that lasted for five days from the 18th up to the 22nd of February, the Ethiopian army was totally destroyed losing its army and weapons.

- On the Halhal front, the Dergue forces were pushed by the subsequent counter offensives of the EPLF. In the Barka and Halhal Fronts, 9,000 enemy troops were killed and wounded and 511 were taken as POWs.

- While the war along Barka and Halhal was raging, intensive fightings were underway in the three Sahel fronts. On the 18th of

190

February, the "Lion of the Jungle" unit (3rd military division) of the Dergue, climbed mount Aget and Mendeat, and tryed to cut-off the road.

- While one military division was mobilized from rear to capture Nakfa. One military division, reinforced with heavy artillery brigades were mobilized along the main front.

- In an attempt to destroy the North Eastern Sahel Front, a military division crossed into the Sudan on the 16$^{th\ of}$ February and another two military divisions were deployed from all directions and an intensive, coordinated and fierce fighting took place.

- Besides defending its frontline from the offensive, the EPLF launched a counter offensive on the right flank of the Northern Eastern Sahel front from 7th to 10th of March. The Dergue army lost 1,500 troops and numerous its weapons were destroyed.

- In addition, on the 24th of March, the EPLF launched another counter offensive against the military division that was taking consecutive attacks crossing through the Sudanese border around Dembobiet, it cleared it out of the positions it had held and was pushed down towards Alakieb.

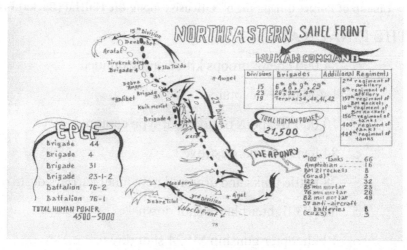

Lineup of Forces during the 6th Offensive along the Northeastern Sahel Front

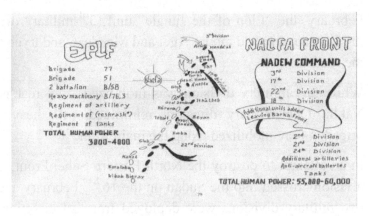

Showing Lineup of Forces during the 6th Offensive along the Nakfa Front

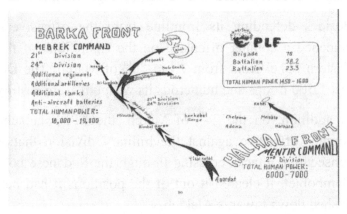

Lineup of Forces during the 6th Offensive along the HalHal (Barka) Front

THE FINAL TALLY

- o 54,000 enemy troops killed and wounded

- o 1,400 troops captured

- o 10,000 weapons of different type captured

- o 84 heavy trucks destroyed

- o 28 battle tanks and armored personnel carriers destroyed

- o 3 MIG fighter planes shot down

- o 1 helicopter gunship MI 24 shot down

On the EPLF side

o 2,700 tegadelti were martyred and 5,000 tegadelti were lightly and heavily wounded.

o The Dergue could not swallow the humiliating defeat of the sixth offensive. As a result and in a quiet way, it soon began to make massive offensive preparations. The Dergue thought that "military capability of the EPLF has been weaken and before the EPLF regains its capability, a sudden and surprise attack could be fruitful." Thus, unlike the sixth offensive, the new offensive was launched stealthily to surprise the Eritrean Revolution. This offensive is duly named by the EPLF as "the stealth offensive". The stealth offensive began at a time when the EPLF had not fully regained from the sixth offensive and had exacted heavy causalities. In addition to these, the enemy forces had better fighting tactics and good choice of terrain and all these added up, made the offensive as challenging as the sixth offensive. The Dergue lost 25,000 troops in the offensive that had lasted up to mid August, 1983. The failure of the Stealth Offensive eventually weakened the Ethiopian forces that had hoped to destroy the Eritrean Revolution with all its resources and power.

Questions

1. Mention all kinds of preparations carried out by the Dergue for the sixth offensive?
2. Explain the outcome of the "Red Star Campaign".

Lesson 40:

Question and Discussion Period

Discussion in groups
- Every classroom forms groups, with each group electing a chairperson and secretary and discussing on assigned topics. A summary of the discussion is then presented to the class.
- Assuming a period is 60 minutes long, 25 minutes are allocated for the discussion part and the remaining 35 minutes for the group presentations.

Points for discussion (to be answered in groups):

1. Discuss whether the decision to make a strategic withdrawal was a correct decision or not and why.
2. Discuss whether the civil war between the ELF and EPLF was avoidable.
3. Discuss the role of the base area in the success of the protracted peoples' war.
4. EPLF's how the popular slogan: "no matter how big the invading army, it will be consumed by flame of the Revolution" represented the nationalist feelings (psyche) of tegadelti and the Eritrean people. Discuss the role of a psychological preparation to achieve victory by take into consideration the sixth offensive as a case.

Lesson 41:

Transition of Eritrean Revolution towards an Offensive Phase (1984 – 1987)

Lesson Goals

At the end of this lesson; students are expected to gain basic knowledge about the following points:

- The role of the confrontations of 1978 – 1983, in transitioning the Eritrean Revolution from a defensive to an offensive mode.

- The capture of the towns of Alighidr, Tessenie, Barentu, the destruction of the Wukaw Command (North Eastern Sahel Front), the commando operation at the Asmara Air Force base.

- Cultural activities of the EPLF

- Global military experience conventional warfare has three phases. In the first phase, the one who have the upper hand launches (to achieve certain objective) an offensive while the other side defends. If the offensive force is weakened in the process and is reduced to the level of the defensive force, a stage where no one has an upper hand is reached. This second stage is called a **Stalemate**. After sometime the balance of power again shifts to one or the other side and the one with the upper hand launches an offensive finishing the war in victory.

- In the period after the strategic withdrawal up to 1983, the Ethiopian colonial army was in the offensive, while the Eritrean Revolution was on the defensive. The enemy forces strategic goal was to defeat the Eritrean Revolution once and for all. Despite conducting seven successive offensives, it could not succeed. The

Eritrean Revolution was able to successfully foil the offensives, however, before turning towards an offensive it had to strengthen its force.

- For the Eritrean Revolution the defensive phase was of paramount importance in transitioning into the offensive phase. The EPLF had garnered an adequate strength for its offensive phase from its defensive phase and the stalemate that followed in 1984. Hence, in the experience of the Eritrean Revolution, it can be said that the stalemate period was the period where the Revolution laid the basis for the transition into the offensive stage. As an illustration to this, the EPLF attacked & liberated Tessenie and Alighidr in January of 1984. Again on 22 February of 1984, EPLF launched an attack on the colonial army that was garrisoned in the Northern Sahel Front for over five years. The enemy army was known by the Amharic name *"Wuqaw Ez" (Wuqaw Command),* which literally means the Threshing Command. Even though, the first attack of the EPLF didn't succeed, in the second attack, which was conducted between 19 and 21 March, the EPLA managed to destroy the entire front and capture the entire area. In this attack the enemy lost around 7,000 soldiers, and over four-fifth of its military hardware that was located in the front was captured.

- Two months after the destruction of the *Wuqaw Command*, EPLF commando unit executed an operation that was unique in its organization and intelligence with devastating and precise destruction of 33 war planes inside the Asmara Air Force base. This operation was a source of pride and key in creating a renewed feeling of optimism in the Eritrean population and it was a shock and brought shame to the enemy creating a feeling of defeat. It was unique and a remarkable operation in the history of the armed struggle.

- In addition to this, the EPLF was conducting special penetrating raids deep behind enemy lines especially in the western part of

Eritrea. As a culmination these penetrating raids, the EPLF carried out an attack on Barentu in July 5, 1985 and liberated the town. The Dergue was considering Barentu as a symbol of resilience and could not accept loosing the it forever. The Dergue regrouped and brought forces from far places like the Ogaden and managed to recapture Barentu, Tessenei and Alighidir after several attempts.

- After the battle of Barentu, the Dergue launched its eighth and last offensive: *"operation Bahri Negash"* on October 10, 1985. After two consecutive attacks and a loss of 17,000 soldiers, the offensive came to an end. There after the EPLF launched a widened guerrilla and commando operations in many corners of the country. These operations on their part continuously engaged the enemy and hindered it from regrouping and conducting another massive military operation or taking initiatives.

Cultural Activities

- The EPLF from its inception had taken the cultural activities as part and parcel of the armed struggle and had been working on it. Especially after the strategic withdrawal from 1979 onwards, the cultural activities that were allowed to mushroom throughout the organization were a big leap forward in building a new national culture. Music, theater, literature and artistic groups were established. Many books were translated from other languages; trainings that upgrade tegadelti's artistic skills and knowledge were conducted.

- During the period when the EPLF was transitioning into the offensive phase, wide cultural activities were carried out in the field and abroad. In the field, beside regular cultural activities that were being conducted at the unit level, grand **cultural festivals** were organized. For example on September 1, 1986, on the occasion of the silver anniversary of the *start of the armed* *struggle*, a grand cultural festival was conducted in the presence of nationals and friends of the Eritrean Revolution.

- An International Symposium on research and development aimed at laying the foundation and developing future Eritrea's education and research was conducted in July 1988.

- Such activities were not limited to the field. Efforts were made to organize Eritrean communities in the Diaspora. These communities, in addition to supporting the Eritrean Revolution, were instrumental in fostering national identity and culture. The annual Bologna Festival in Italy which started in the early 1980s was a typical examples of such successful cultural events carried out abroad.

Eritrean Festival in Bologna

Questions

1. Elaborate the difference between the stalemate and offensive phases.
2. List the developments that show the transition from a stalemate to an offensive phase.

Lesson 42:

Second and Unity Congress

Lesson Goals:

At the end of this lesson; students are expected to gain basic knowledge about the following points:

- The process of unity between the EPLF and ELF – Central Leadership (SAGIM)
- Second and unity Congress
- The National Democratic program and the organizational structure of the EPLF that was amended and approved in the second congress
- Political Resolutions of the Congress

- Second and Unity Congress, as its name implies, was not only the 2nd EPLF's Congress but also a Congress for Unity. As already stated in previous lessons, the ELF, after it was forced to pushed into the Sudan, had disintegrated and was fragmented into many factions and organizations. One of the organizations that were formed after the disintegration of the ELF was the ELF Central Leadership (SAGIM). Starting 1983, the two organizations namely the EPLF and SAGIM were discussing about unity. After they reached a unity agreement, SAGIM forces, which were limited to the camps in the Sudan came back to the field in June 11, 1983. In the ensuing years, a common program was issued and implemented by both sides.

- After two years both organizations agreed to be united. Hence the relationship of the two organizations reached a complete unity in the Second and Unity Congress.

Second and Unity Congress of the EPLF and ELF-CL

- The EPLF was supposed to conduct its congress two years after the first congress. As stated in the previous lessons, the EPLF was in a heavy engagement and could not conduct its congress as per its program. In 1986, as the enemy was weakened, the EPLF got the opportunity to organize the Second and Unity Congress

- Before conducting the Congress: a committee prepared draft constitution and an amended National Democratic Program and disseminated it for discussion among the tegadelti and mass organizations. Report on the ten years experience of 1977 to 1987 was also disseminated for discussion. After the completion of the necessary preparations, the Second and Unity Congress between the EPLF and ELF Central Leadership (SAGM) was conducted from 12 to 19 March 1987.

- In the Congress 1,287 democratically elected representatives of tegadelti and civilians, Mr. Woldeab Woldemariam, Mr. Ibrahim Sultan, nationalist organizations such as the ELF-RC, ELF-PLF Unified Organization, and individuals were present. Representatives of 25 governments, parties and organizations,

200

representatives of Eritrean support committees read their messages in person and another 50 sent their messages to the Congress.

- In the congress Mr. Woldeab Woldemariam in person, and Sheik Ibrahim Sultan via video passed sensational messages that touched the hearts of the participants.

> *"**Natsinet (independence) if** it is stated by its nationals and in their native language as 'Natsinet' it is enough. In order for independence to be independence, it doesn't not need and is not necessary to be called independence...., Liberta ...., ... in foreign languages. The core point of Natsinet is its presence or absence. If its existence is confirmed, whether it is blessed or not been blessed by foreigners is immaterial. .... The Eritrean public, by its own will and strength has put the crown of independence, woe unto him who dares touch this crown......*

> Sheik Ibrahim Sultan on his part called for unity using the simple phrase: *"my fellow countrymen, be in one accord."*

In general in the congress:

- Political reports of the two organizations were presented
- Congress participants discussed and approved all the articles of the political programs and constitution of the organization.
- Passed resolutions on important national, neighboring countries and global issues
- A Central Committee mandated to lead up to the third congress, comprised of 71 permanent and 7 alternative

members was elected. In turn the Central Committee elected Isaias Afwerki as the Secretary General of the Organization and nine members (including Isaias) to form the politburo of the EPLF.

Isaias Afwerki, EPLF Secretary General 1987 -1994

In the second congress, changes were made on the EPLF's organizational structure and its political programs. To state some of the paramount contents of the National Democratic Program:

1. Establish People's Democratic Government.

 a) Destroy colonialist Ethiopia's administrative organs and system of administration, and annulling any agreement signed on issues dealing with Eritrea regarding military, economic, political and cultural agreements.

 b) Establish government that keeps the interest of the masses and not serve the interest of foreign powers.

c) Establish a freely elected people's assembly that drafts the constitution, draws laws, elects the judiciary and executive organs.

d) Rights to free expression, free assembly, free peaceful demonstration, and freedom of religion.

Furthermore, the program accepted political pluralism and guaranteed the establishment of national political parties and other associations.

1. Establish a government free from foreign control and follow a system of planned mixed economy that enables the participation of government and private sector, based on the principles of self-reliance.

2. Follow a peaceful and non-aligned foreign policy.

Resolutions of the Congress

- To confirm the unity of the Eritrean people: the EPLF has confirmed its readiness of establishing a National Democratic Front of the masses by gathering the national forces, groups and individuals;

- It underlined its readiness to peace negotiations that was based on the right of the Eritrean people for self determination. Bring peace and stability to the Horn of Africa without conflicting people's right for self determination, proposed to create a political environment based on common interest to the peoples of Somalia, Djibouti, Ethiopia, Sudan and Eritrea.

- The EPLF believing that a military coup d'état can't be a replacement to people's government, if the Ethiopian army by ousting the Dergue establishes a democratic environment, and is ready to surrender power to the people, accepts the right of the

Eritrean people for self determination, confirms its readiness to solve the Eritrean case peaceful, then the EPLF gives its assurance for a ceasefire.

Questions

1. Why was the Organizational Congress held in 1987, named as Second and Unity Congress?
2. List the changes made in the organizational structure and programs of the EPLF in the Second and Unity Congress.

Lesson 43:

Strategic Offensive Phase of the Eritrean Revolution (1988 – 1991)

Lesson Goals:

At the end of this lesson; students are expected to gain basic knowledge about the following points:

- The strategic significance of the destruction of the "Nadew Command"
- The Eritrean Revolution in between Nadew and Fenkel
- Operation Fenkel
- The final push for the liberation of all of Eritrea
- Peace negotiations with the Dergue and the principled stand of the EPLF

After the Second and Unity congress, the EPLF facilitated its work in all aspects. As an illustration to this, in the year 1987 alone, 168 military confrontations were carried out. Most of these military operations were behind enemy lines. These confrontations, besides leaving scars over the Dergue army, they were key in clearing the road for the strategic offensive of the revolution that followed.

Destruction of "Nadew Command": The Dien Bien Phu of Eritrea

- Destruction of "Nadew Command" which occurred after the Second and Unity Congress was one of the biggest strategic offensives that tipped the balance of power in favor of the Eritrean Revolution. The "Nadew Command" (The Amharic word Nadew

205

literally means "destroy it") stationed at Nakfa and Afabiet fronts for nine years had 22,000 soldiers. The EPLA, prior to launching the offensive that destroyed the Nadew Command, had conducted a tactical attack in December 1987 to strengthen its position.

- After a meticulous and secretive preparation, the EPLA launched its offensive against the "Nadew Command" from 17 to 19 March 1988 from three flanks. **Left Flank:** attacked from the side of coastal area, blocking the Feleket Valley, Sheleb and Azhara and cutting off enemy forces who were attempting to escape from Afabet to the East. **Central Flank:** carried out a surprise attack on enemy trenches on the side of Hiday River. In the **Right Flank**, the EPLF attacked the enemy trenches of the 18th Division. There was also an EPLF attack that came from behind enemy line that cut the Afabiet - Keren road.

Destruction of the Nadew Command at Afabet

- As planned, the EPLA liberated the town of Afabet within 48 hours, in the morning hours of March 19. The Dergue out of its 22,000 experienced soldiers, lost 18,000 as POWs, wounded or killed (that was 20% of the total Dergue army). For the first time, three Soviet military advisors; (two colonels and one lieutenant), who were actively participating in the war were captured. 50 tanks, 100 trucks, 60 heavy artilleries, 20 anti aircraft artillery and tens of thousands light weapons became the property of the Eritrean Revolution.

- As a result of the Nadew offensive and the attacks launched by the EPLF at Hal-Hal front, the Dergue pulled out of Tessenei, Barentu & Akurdet and decided to establish a garrison narrowly in the northern part of Keren, thus entering into a state of defensive mode.

- Basil Davidson; the renowned researcher of African history and author, in his interview with the BBC through a satellite telephone from the field described the destruction of the Nadew Command as "One of the biggest ever scored by a liberation movement anywhere since Dien Bien Phu[3]". In reality the Nadew Offensive was not only a step forward in changing the military balance of power; but also a turning point with a huge political & propaganda gain for the just struggle of the Eritrean people.

- In addition, the EPLA, established a small unit equipped with fast boats that started confronting the experienced and relatively big colonial Ethiopia's Navy in the sea. For example, on 19 April 1988, an attack was launched on Assab, damaging the refinery and an Ethiopian Navy ship. On the same year on May 31, an attack was carried out using fast boats and destroying two Ethiopian ships which were on the narrow straits of Massawa. On September

---

[3]The Battle of Dien Bien Phuwas the finalbattle between the Viet Minh nationalist revolutionaries and the French colonial army that went on from 1946 through 1954. This battle in Dien Bien Phua city in north western Vietnam between March and May of 1954 culminated in a comprehensive French defeat influencingthe French to come to negotiations over the future of Indochina.

6, that same year attacks were carried out on the port of Massawa and destroying 3 big ships and the enemy's stores.

- In retaliation to these heavy losses, the Dergue declared a "State of Emergency" and started committing more atrocities against the civilian population. On May 12, 1988, in Sheeb, the Dergue massacred 400 innocent civilian women, children and the elderly by crushing them under tank chains. The Dergue continued its atrocities on the peaceful civilian population in places like Shebah, Gogeitay and Semienawi Bahri, and Rora Mensae.

- The EPLA's launching of big offensives against the Dergue assisted Ethiopian opposition organizations. The EPLF, to preserve & sustain its victories, continued its cooperation with Ethiopian opposition organizations and signed agreements of military assistance. (With the TPLF in April 1988 and the OLF in March 1988).

The Eritrean Revolution between Nadew and Fenkel

- To sustain the momentum gained by the destruction of Nadew, and to accelerate and maintain its pressure on the enemy, the EPLF increased its attack on different trenches of the enemy. In April 1988, it launched a wide unsuccessful offensive in Keren front. Again in May 1988, the EPLF launched another unsuccessful offensive in the same front.

- The Dergue after stabilizing its position in the Keren Front and to ease the pressure it was facing from the EPLA, tried to recapture Afabet by opening a front in the plains of Azhara and Maamide. The EPLA foiled the offensive and improved its position by opening a limited tactical attack in the Mensae front.

- In the second half of 1988, the naval force of the Eritrean People's Liberation Army launched military operations over the Dergue's naval force garrisoned in the gulf of Massawa targeting its Naval Assets.

- The EPLA was not able to break through the Keren front in two prior offensives. For this reason, it made a tactical shift and set its focus on the eastern plains (Semhar province, presently named as the Northern Red Sea Region). Beginning in 1989, a commando unit carried out a mechanized operation in the northern plains of Semhar as an example of this new tactical plan.

- Other important EPLA military operations were the joint operations with the TPLF and OLF in Shire (Tigray, northern Ethiopia) and Asosa (Welega, western Ethiopia). The Shire offensive was a huge victory that compelled the Dergue to completely pull its army out of Tigray.

- These victorious attacks in addition to their political significance (reflected the friendship the EPLF forged with Ethiopian opposition organizations), weakened the military capability of the Dergue, confused the military intelligence of the Dergue and enabled the surprise Fenkel offensive. Surprise attacks play paramount role in victorious offensives.

- In general, in the period between the destruction of Nadew and operation Fenkel, 50 moderate and big battles were conducted. These battles cleared the way for the liberation of Massawa.

Operation Fenkil: Gateway to Liberation

- After one year of preparation, the EPLF started to secretly garrison its units around Semhar. The offensive started on February 8, 1990. One side of the offensive was along the Asmara – Massawa road, cutting off around Gahtelay extending up toward Dongollo. The other side of the offensive was penetrating through the plains of Semhar to liberate Massawa.

EPLF Launches Operation Fenkil to Liberate Massawa

- In the second day of the offensive, the EPLA reached in the vicinity of Massawa. The EPLF navy using fast boats destroyed most of the Ethiopian warships of the naval force. After three days of battle, the EPLA controlled all of Massawa. Massawa was liberated and the colonial government of Ethiopia entered into desperate and critical state.

- After the liberation of Massawa, the Dergue in retaliation of its defeat the Ethiopian air force bombed the civilian population of Massawa using cluster and napalm bombs. Hundreds of civilians were killed, grain stores were burned and the already damaged infrastructure of the port met a huge destruction.

- The Fenkel Offensive for the liberation of Massawa was extensive in terms of size and scope. It had a shock effect to the Dergue, it hastened the final defeat of colonial Ethiopia, it lifted the status of the Eritrean Revolution in global stages and introduced the Revolution as a regional force that can't be neglected.

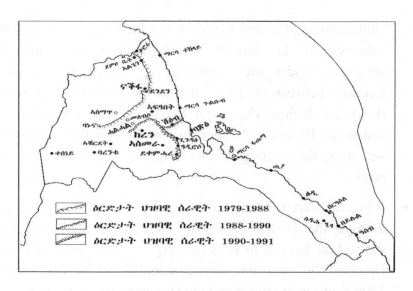

EPLA Trenches 1979 – 1991

First Stage (1979-1988) was 667 km long,
Second Stage (1988-1990) was 300 km long
Final Stage (1990-1991) was 415 km long

Negotiations for a peaceful Solution "A Right that don't allow any Compromise"

- The EPLF had a clear and principled stand on peaceful procedures to solve the Eritrean issue. It was ready to participate in any peace talks that was based on the right of the Eritrean people for self determination. As an illustration to its readiness to solve the Eritrean issue through peaceful processes, in 1980, EPLF came up with the Referendum Proposal. However, as the Dergue wasn't ready for a genuine peace, and the armed struggle of the Eritrean people had to continue.

- After the offensive to destroy Nadew Command and the shifting of the balance of power in favor of the Eritrean Revolution and the unsuccessful military coup d'état to overthrown Mengistu by his highest military commanders in May 1989, many countries started engagement attempting to solve the Eritrean case. Under such

211

circumstance of global focus for the Eritrean case, the focus and initiative of the former American president Jimmy Carter appeared. Under the mediation of Carter, two consecutive meetings between the EPLF and the Dergue were held in Atlanta (USA) and Nairobi (Kenya) in September and November 1989 in that order. However, the meetings were not fruitful as the Dergue was using the meetings to buy time, not as a genuine interest for peace.

- When the Carter initiative failed and the EPLF liberated Massawa through the Fenkel offensive, the United States of America showed an interest to start meetings between the EPLF and the Dergue. With such initiative, a meeting was held on October 4, 1990 between the EPLF and the Dergue in the State Department of the United States of America. It was apparent that this meeting and subsequent meetings in Washington and London were not out of consideration for the basic right of the Eritrean People for self determination, but aimed at saving the Dergue. They did not consider the military developments on the ground, and as a result could not bear any fruit. In the mean time the whole Eritrea was liberated.

Last Push for the Liberation of Eritrea

- After Operation Fenkel, heavy confrontations were carried out by the Dergue to recapture lost territory and by the EPLF to preserve its victories. The confrontations of Ghindae and Bizen can be taken as such examples. The EPLF evaluated the unlikely possibility to go beyond Ghindae front towards Asmara; it then shifted to the South and launched an offensive at the end of April 1990. Within two months the towns of Senafe, Adi Keih and Segeniety were liberated.

- To recapture lost territory, the Dergue made several unsuccessful incursions. Even though attacks were launched in Ghindae, Bizen, and Hal-Hal fronts, the Dergue could not succeed.

- After offensives and counter offensives for a year, the EPLF started to conduct the final offensives in February of 1991 to finish the war. As a result, Tio and Edi were liberated and on May 19, 1991 Dekemhare was liberated and on May 24, 1991, Asmara was liberated.

EPLA on the streets of AsmaraCelebrating Liberation in Asmara

- Full Liberation of Eritrea took place with the liberation of Assab on May 26, 1991. Eritrea was liberated and Ethiopian colonialism came to an end. The EPRDF through decisive military support of the EPLF finished victoriously the Ethiopian offensives and controlled Addis Ababa.

- The EPLF, based on its conviction to solve the just question of the Eritrean people through peaceful means, had proclaimed the referendum proposal as early as 1980. This announcement was based on the international law that demands for oppressed people the right for self determination. It is mainly for this reason that after the liberation, Eritrea established a Provisional Government and announced to conduct a referendum in two years. The decision to conduct a referendum was to make the liberation that was achieved militarily, legal through the ballot box. As planned, the referendum was held from April 23 to 25, 1993. Out of 1,102,410

Eritrean voters, 99.8% voted yes for independence. Eritrea became a free and sovereign nation.

Questions

1. Elaborate the military and political significance of the destruction of Nadew Command.
2. State the military, political and diplomatic benefits of Operation Fenkel to the Eritrean Revolution.
3. Why did the EPLF defer the formal declaration of independence for two years?
4. Clarify the significance and outcome of referendum?

Lesson 44:

Question and Discussion Period

Discussion in groups

- **Every classroom forms groups, with each group electing a chairperson and secretary and discussing on assigned topics. A summary of the discussion is then presented to the class.**

- **Assuming a period is 60 minutes long, 25 minutes are allocated for the discussion part and the remaining 35 minutes for the group presentations.**

Points for discussion (to be answered in groups):

1. Discuss how the defensive phase of the Eritrean Revolution was instrumental in a transition to the offensive phase?

2. In the Second and Unity Congress, amendments were made in the policies and programs of the EPLF. Why is it that an organization has to review its programs continuously?

3. Basil Davidson stated that the destruction of Nadew Command with similar to the battle of Dien Bien Phu. Do you think his comparison was correct? Discuss it.

Made in the USA
Middletown, DE
18 October 2023

41049827R00126